Theme 2

Colors All Around

OBJECTIVES

Phonemic Awareness beginning sounds; syllables in spoken words

Phonics sounds for letters *S, s; M, m; R, r*

High-Frequency Words recognize two new high-frequency words

Reading Strategies predict/infer; summarize; phonics/decoding

Comprehension Skills sequence of events; inferences: making predictions

Vocabulary describing words; exact naming words; singular/plural naming words

Writing description; journals; graphic organzier; class story

Listening/Speaking/Viewing activities to support vocabulary expansion and writing

Theme 2

Colors All Around
Literature Resources

WEEK 1

Teacher Read Aloud
I Need a Lunch Box
fiction by Jeannette Caines
pages T10–T11

Big Book
I Went Walking
concept book by Sue Williams
pages T18–T19, T28–T33

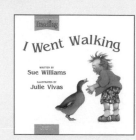

Science Link
What's My Favorite Color?
nonfiction
pages T40–T41

Decodable Phonics Library
My Red Boat
page T35

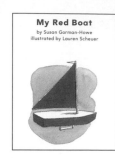

WEEK 2

Teacher Read Aloud
Caps of Many Colors
a traditional tale
pages T62–T65

Big Book
In the Big Blue Sea
nonfiction by Chyng Feng Sun
pages T72–T73, T82–T87

Science Link
What Do You Do, Norbert Wu?
nonfiction
pages T94–T95

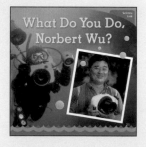

Decodable Phonics Library
Look at Me!
page T89

WEEK 3

Teacher Read Aloud
How the Birds Got Their Colors
pourquoi tale told in North and South America
pages T116–T119

Revisit the Big Books:
I Went Walking
pages T126–T127

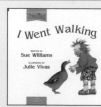

In the Big Blue Sea
pages T136–T137

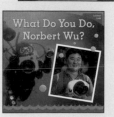

Revisit the Links: Science
What's My Favorite Color?
page T144

Social Studies
What Do You Do, Norbert Wu?
page T145

Decodable Phonics Library
The Parade
page T139

Kindergarten

Teacher's Edition

Senior Authors J. David Cooper, John J. Pikulski

Authors Patricia A. Ackerman, Kathryn H. Au, David J. Chard, Gilbert G. Garcia, Claude N. Goldenberg, Marjorie Y. Lipson, Susan E. Page, Shane Templeton, Sheila W. Valencia, MaryEllen Vogt

Consultants Linda H. Butler, Linnea C. Ehri, Carla B. Ford

HOUGHTON MIFFLIN   BOSTON • MORRIS PLAINS, NJ

California • Colorado • Georgia • Illinois • New Jersey • Texas

Literature Reviewers

Consultants: **Dr. Adela Artola Allen**, Associate Dean, Graduate College, Associate Vice President for Inter-American Relations, University of Arizona, Tucson, Arizona; **Dr. Manley Begay**, Co-director of the Harvard Project on American Indian Economic Development, Director of the National Executive Education Program for Native Americans, Harvard University, John F. Kennedy School of Government, Cambridge, Massachusetts; **Dr. Nicholas Kannellos**, Director, Arte Publico Press, Director, Recovering the U.S. Hispanic Literacy Heritage Project, University of Houston, Texas; **Mildred Lee**, author and former head of Library Services for Sonoma County, Santa Rosa, California; **Dr. Barbara Moy**, Director of the Office of Communication Arts, Detroit Public Schools, Michigan; **Norma Naranjo**, Clark County School District, Las Vegas, Nevada; **Dr. Arlette Ingram Willis**, Associate Professor, Department of Curriculum and Instruction, Division of Language and Literacy, University of Illinois at Urbana-Champaign, Illinois

Teachers: **Helen Brooks**, Vestavia Hills Elementary School, Birmingham, Alabama; **Patricia Buchanan**, Thurgood Marshall School, Newark, Delaware; **Gail Connor**, Language Arts Resource Teacher, Duval County, Jacksonville, Florida; **Vicki DeMott**, McClean Science/Technology School, Wichita, Kansas; **Marge Egenhoffer**, Dixon Elementary School, Brookline, Wisconsin; **Mary Jew Mori**, Griffin Avenue Elementary, Los Angeles, California

Program Reviewers

Supervisors: **Judy Artz**, Middletown Monroe City School District, Ohio; **James Bennett**, Elkhart Schools, Elkhart, Indiana; **Kay Buckner-Seal**, Wayne County, Michigan; **Charlotte Carr**, Seattle School District, Washington; **Sister Marion Christi**, St. Matthews School, Archdiocese of Philadelphia, Pennsylvania; **Alvina Crouse**, Garden Place Elementary, Denver Public Schools, Colorado; **Peggy DeLapp**, Minneapolis, Minnesota; **Carol Erlandson**, Wayne Township Schools, Marion County, Indianapolis; **Brenda Feeney**, North Kansas City School District, Missouri; **Winnie Huebsch**, Sheboygan Area Schools, Wisconsin; **Brenda Mickey**, Winston-Salem/Forsyth County Schools, North Carolina; **Audrey Miller**, Sharpe Elementary School, Camden, New Jersey; **JoAnne Piccolo**, Rocky Mountain Elementary, Adams 12 District, Colorado; **Sarah Rentz**, East Baton Rouge Parish School District, Louisiana; **Kathy Sullivan**, Omaha Public Schools, Nebraska; **Rosie Washington**, Kuny Elementary, Gary, Indiana; **Theresa Wishart**, Knox County Public Schools, Tennessee

Teachers: **Carol Brockhouse**, Madison Schools, Wayne Westland Schools, Michigan; **Eva Jean Conway**, R.C. Hill School, Valley View School District, Illinois; **Carol Daley**, Jane Addams School, Sioux Falls, South Dakota; **Karen Landers**, Watwood Elementary, Talladega County, Alabama; **Barb LeFerrier**, Mullenix Ridge Elementary, South Kitsap District, Port Orchard, Washington; **Loretta Piggee**, Nobel School, Gary, Indiana; **Cheryl Remash**, Webster Elementary School, Manchester, New Hampshire; **Marilynn Rose**, Michigan; **Kathy Scholtz**, Amesbury Elementary School, Amesbury, Massachusetts; **Dottie Thompson**, Erwin Elementary, Jefferson County, Alabama; **Dana Vassar**, Moore Elementary School, Winston-Salem, North Carolina; **Joy Walls**, Ibraham Elementary School, Winston-Salem, North Carolina; **Elaine Warwick**, Fairview Elementary, Williamson County, Tennessee

Credits

Cover
Copyright © Sunstar/International Stock

Theme Opener
(t) Robin Prange/The Stock Market, (tm) Bob Winsett/IndexStock, (bm) copyright © Sunstar/International Stock, (b) Andre Jenny/Focus Group/PictureQuest

Assignment Photography
Joel Benjamin
pp. xiv, xv, T6, T13, T43, T58, T67, T75, T77, T97, T121, T129

Illustration
Lydia Dabcovich, p. T65; Francisco Mora, p. T118

Acknowledgments

Grateful acknowledgment is made for permission to reprint copyrighted material as follows:

Theme 2
I Went Walking, by Sue Williams, illustrated by Julie Vivas. Text copyright © 1989 by Sue Williams. Illustrations copyright © 1989 by Julie Vivas. Reprinted by permission of Harcourt Inc.

Lodge
Textbook
PE
1119
H68
'2001
Gr. K
TE
Th. 2

Big Books for Use All Year

From Apples to Zebras: A Book of ABC's

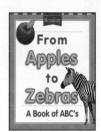

Higglety Pigglety: A Book of Rhymes

Leveled Books

See Cumulative Listing of Leveled Books.

Phonics Library

Decodable

- My Red Boat
- Look at Me!
- The Parade

Lessons, pages T35, T89, T139

On My Way Practice Reader

Easy / **On Level**

Beautiful Butterflies
by Demaris Tyler
page T153

Little Big Books

On Level / **Challenge**

I Went Walking

In the Big Blue Sea

🔊 Audiotape

Colors All Around

Houghton Mifflin Classroom Bookshelf

Level K

Little Readers for Guided Reading

Collection K

Bibliography

Key

 Science

 Social Studies

 Multicultural

 Music

 Math

 Classic

 Art

Books for Browsing

 Green
by Mary Elizabeth Salzmann
Sandcastle 1999 (24p)
Photos and simple text describe familiar objects that are the color green. See others in series.

 Freight Train
by Donald Crews
Greenwillow 1978 (24p)
A train of colored cars journeys through tunnels, by cities, and over trestles.

 Yellow Ball
by Molly Bang
Morrow 1991 (24p) also paper
A boy's yellow ball drifts out to sea and washes up on a distant shore.

 Carmen's Colors
by Maria Diaz Strom
Lee & Low (8p) 2000
A Mexican American girl and her mother buy an array of colorful items at an outdoor market.

 Color Dance
by Ann Jonas
Greenwillow 1989 (32p)
A dancer waving a scarf demonstrates different color combinations.

Tell Me a Season*
by Mary McKenna Siddals
Clarion 1997 (32p)
Simple text describes the colors of the changing seasons.

 Butterfly Colors
by Helen Frost
Pebble 1999 (24p)
Photographs present the colors and patterns of butterfly wings.

Colors Everywhere
by Tana Hoban
Greenwillow 1995 (32p)
Vibrant photographs reveal the many colors found in ordinary objects.

 Kente Colors
by Debbi Chocolate
Walker 1996 (32p) also paper
A celebration of the traditional, colorful kente cloth made by the peoples of Ghana and Togo.

 Planting a Rainbow
by Lois Ehlert
Harcourt 1988 (32p) also paper
Planting a garden of flowers, a child learns the colors of the rainbow.

Mouse Paint
by Ellen Stoll Walsh
Harcourt 1989 (32p) also paper
Three white mice experiment with jars of red, yellow, and blue paint.
Available in Spanish as *Pinta ratones.*

Books for Teacher Read Aloud

 Harold and the Purple Crayon
by Robert Kraus
Harper 1955 (64p) also paper
A boy draws himself exciting adventures with a purple crayon.
Available in Spanish as *Harold y el lápiz color morado.*

 A Color of His Own
by Leo Lionni
Knopf paper 1997 (32p)
A chameleon goes in search of a color he can call his very own.

 All the Colors of the Earth
by Sheila Hamanaka
Morrow 1994 (32p)
Young people of all colors dance across the pages of this poetic celebration of diversity.

Lilly's Purple Plastic Purse
by Kevin Henkes
Greenwillow 1996 (32p)
The new purple plastic purse Lilly takes to school gets her into trouble.

 Mr. Rabbit and the Lovely Present
by Charlotte Zolotow
Harper 1962 (32p) also paper
A rabbit helps a girl create a colorful birthday gift for her mother.
Available in Spanish as *El señor Conejo y el hermoso regalo.*

 Animals Black and White
by Phyllis Limbacher Tildes
Charlesbridge 1996 (32p) also paper
Questions and answers present information on black-and-white animals.

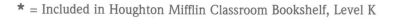
* = Included in Houghton Mifflin Classroom Bookshelf, Level K

Chidi Only Likes Blue
by Ifeoma Onyefulu
Dutton 1997 (32p) also paper
Chidi's older sister teaches him
about the colors they see in their
Nigerian village.

George Paints His House
by Francine Bassède
Orchard 1999 (32p)
George the duck's animal friends
give him ideas on what color to
paint his house.

Books for Shared Reading

A Beasty Story
by Bill Martin Jr
Harcourt 1999 (32p)
In a rhyming story incorporating
color words, four mice who explore
a dark house get a surprise.

 Mary Wore Her Red Dress and Henry Wore His Green Sneakers*
by Merle Peek
Clarion 1985 (32p) also paper
On Katy's birthday
her animal friends
come to the party
dressed in clothes
of different colors.

Brown Bear, Brown Bear, What Do You See?
by Bill Martin Jr
Holt 1992 (32p)
Animals answer the repeated
question "What do you see?"
in a playful book about color.

 One Gray Mouse
by Katherine Burton
Kids Can 1997 (32p)
Readers count from one gray
mouse to ten red snails in this
rhyme.

Teeny, Tiny Mouse
by Laura Leuck
Bridgewater 1998 (32p)
A teeny, tiny mouse names
objects of various colors he
sees around his house.

My Crayons Talk
by Patricia Hubbard
Holt 1996 (32p)
Rhyming verse celebrates color
as a child imagines her crayons
talking.

 Let's Go Visiting
by Sue Williams
Harcourt 1998 (32p)
A boy visits his farmyard friends,
from one brown foal to six yellow
puppies.

New Shoes, Red Shoes
by Susan Rollings
Orchard 2000 (32p)
Bouncy verse tells how a girl
goes shopping for a new pair
of shoes with her mother.

Books for Phonics Read Aloud

 A Rainbow of My Own
by Don Freeman
Puffin 1978 (32p)
A small boy who longs to have
a rainbow of his own has his
wish fulfilled.

Miss Mary Mack
by Mary Ann Hoberman
Little 1998 (32p)
A purple elephant jumps over a
fence with funny consequences.

Who Said Red?
by Mary Serfozo
McElderry 1988 (32p)
As a girl suggests colors he might
like, a boy looks for his red kite in
this rhyming story.

* = Included in Houghton Mifflin Classroom Bookshelf, Level K

Computer Software Resources

- **Curious George® Learns Phonics**
- **Lexia Quick Phonics Assessment**
- **Lexia Phonics Intervention CD-ROM: Primary**
- **Published by Sunburst Technology***
  Tenth Planet™ Vowels: Short and Long
  Curious George® Pre-K ABCs
  First Phonics
- **Published by The Learning Company**
  Dr. Seuss's ABC™

Video Cassettes

- **Harold and the Purple Crayon** *by Robert Krauss. Weston Woods*
- **Dr. Seuss's My Many Colored Days** *by Dr. Seuss. Weston Woods*
- **The Red Balloon** *by Albert Lamorisse. Weston Woods*
- **All the Colors of the Earth** *by Sheila Hamanaka. Weston Woods*
- **A Rainbow of My Own** *by Don Freeman. Weston Woods*
- **Freight Train** *by Donald Crews. SRA Media*

Audio Cassettes

- **Mary Wore Her Red Dress and Henry Wore His Sneakers** *by Merle Peek. Houghton*
- **Art Dog** *by Thacher Hurd. Live Oak*
- **Caps for Sale** *by Esphyr Slobodkina. Live Oak*
- **Mr. Rabbit and the Lovely Present** *by Charlotte Zolotow. Live Oak*
- **Henry and Mudge Under the Yellow Moon** *by Cynthia Rylant. Live Oak*
- **Audiotapes for *Colors All Around Us.*** *Houghton Mifflin Company*

* © Sunburst Technology Corporation, a Houghton Mifflin Company. All Rights Reserved.
Technology Resources addresses are on page R8.

Education Place
www.eduplace.com *Log on to Education Place for more activities relating to* Colors All Around.
Book Adventure
www.bookadventure.org *This Internet reading incentive program provides thousands of titles for students to read.*

Theme 2

Theme at a Glance

Theme Concept: *We see beautiful colors everywhere.*

☑ **Indicates Tested Skills**

Learning to Read

	Phonemic Awareness and Phonics	High-Frequency Words	Comprehension Skills and Strategies
WEEK 1 **Read Aloud** **I Need A Lunch Box** **Big Book** **I Went Walking** **Science Link** **What's My Favorite Color?** **Phonics Library** *"My Red Boat"* 	☑ Phonemic Awareness: Beginning Sounds, *T9, T17, T27, T39, T47* ☑ Syllables in Spoken Words, *T9, T17, T27, T39, T47* ☑ Initial Consonant *s, T12–T13, T20–T21* ☑ Review Initial Consonant *s, T34, T42–T43* Phonics Review: Familiar Consonants; *s, T13, T20, T36, T44, T50, T52*	☑ High-Frequency Words, *T22–T23, T35, T51* Word Wall, *T26, T38, T46*	☑ Comprehension: Sequence of Events, *T10, T18, T29, T31, T32, T40, T48* Strategies: Predict/Infer, *T10, T18, T29, T30, T40* Phonics/Decoding, *T35*
WEEK 2 **Read Aloud** **Caps of Many Colors** **Big Book** **In the Big Blue Sea** **Science Link** **What Do You Do, Norbert Wu?** **Phonics Library** *"Look at Me!"* 	☑ Phonemic Awareness: Beginning Sounds, *T61, T71, T81, T93, T101* ☑ Syllables in Spoken Words, *T61, T71, T81, T93, T101* ☑ Initial Consonant *m, T66–T67, T74–T75* ☑ Review Initial Consonant *m, T88, T96–T97* Phonics Review: Familiar Consonants; *m, s, T67, T74, T90, T98, T104, T106*	☑ High-Frequency Words, *T76–T77, T89, T105* Word Wall, *T60, T70, T80, T92, T100*	☑ Comprehension: Inferences: Making Predictions, *T62, T72, T83, T85, T94, T102* Strategies: Summarize, *T62, T72, T83, T84, T94* Phonics/Decoding, *T89*
WEEK 3 **Read Aloud** **How the Birds Got Their Colors** **Big Books** **I Went Walking** **In the Big Blue Sea** **Science Links** **What's My Favorite Color?** **What Do You Do, Norbert Wu?** **Phonics Library** *"The Parade"* 	☑ Phonemic Awareness: Beginning Sounds, *T115, T125, T135, T143, T151* ☑ Syllables in Spoken Words, *T115, T125, T135, T143, T151* ☑ Initial Consonant *r, T120–T121, T128–T129* ☑ Review Initial Consonant *r, T138, T146–T147* Phonics Review: Familiar Consonants; *m, s, r, T121, T128, T140, T148, T154, T156*	High-Frequency Words, *T130–T131, T139, T155* Word Wall, *T114, T124, T134, T142, T150*	☑ Comprehension: Sequence of Events, *T116, T127, T144, T152* ☑ Inferences: Making Predictions, *T126, T136, T144, T145, T152* Strategies: Predict/Infer, *T116, T126, T144* Summarize, *T136, T137, T145* Phonics/Decoding, *T139*

Pacing	Multi–age Classroom	Technology 
• This theme is designed to take approximately 3 weeks, depending on your students' needs.	**Related theme—** • **Grade 1:** *Let's Look Around*	**Education Place: www.eduplace.com** Log on to Education Place for more activities relating to *Colors All Around*. **Lesson Planner CD-ROM:** Customize your planning for *Colors All Around* with the Lesson Planner.

Word Work		Writing & Language			Centers
High-Frequency Word Practice	**Exploring Words**	**Oral Language**	**Writing**	**Listening/ Speaking/Viewing**	**Content Areas**
Exploring Words, *T14, T24*	Color Words, *T36, T44, T52*	**Using Describing Words** • picture and color word cards, *T15* **Vocabulary Expansion** • using describing words, *T25*	**Shared Writing** • writing a description, *T37* **Interactive Writing** • writing a description, *T45* **Independent Writing** • Journals, *T53*	Viewing and Speaking, *T25, T37, T45*	Book Center, *T11* Phonics Center, *T13, T21, T43* Writing Center, *T15, T45* Science Center, *T19* Art Center, *T25, T33*
Matching Words, *T68* Building Sentences, *T78*	Color Words, *T90, T98, T106*	**Using Exact Naming Words** • naming word chart, *T69* **Vocabulary Expansion** • using exact naming words, *T79*	**Shared Writing** • writing a description, *T91* **Interactive Writing** • writing a description, *T99* **Independent Writing** • Journals, *T107*	Listening and Speaking, *T69* Viewing and Speaking, *T79, T91*	Book Center, *T79* Phonics Center, *T67, T75, T97* Writing Center, *T69* Dramatic Play Center, *T63* Science Center, *T73* Art Center, *T87*
Matching Words, *T122* Building Sentences, *T132*	Color Words, *T140, T148, T156*	**Using Singular and Plural Words** • naming words, *T123* **Vocabulary Expansion** • using plural names, *T133*	**Shared Writing** • writing a graphic organizer, *T141* **Interactive Writing** • writing a class story, *T149* **Independent Writing** • Journals, *T157*	Viewing and Speaking, *T123, T133*	Book Center, *T112* Phonics Center, *T121, T129, T147* Writing Center, *T123* Dramatic Play Center, *T117* Science Center, *T127, T137, T145* Art Center, *T133*

Planning for Assessment

Use these resources to meet your assessment needs. For additional information, see the *Teacher's Assessment Handbook*.

Emerging Literacy Survey

Diagnostic Planning

Emerging Literacy Survey

- If you have used this survey to obtain baseline data on the skills children brought with them to kindergarten, this might be a good time to re-administer all or parts of the survey to chart progress, to identify areas of strength and need, and to test the need for early intervention.

Ongoing Assessment

Phonemic Awareness:

- **Practice Book,** pp. 47–48, 57–58, 67–68

Phonics:

- **Practice Book,** pp. 49, 52, 59, 62, 69, 71

Comprehension:

- **Practice Book** Reading Responses, pp. 45–46, 51, 55–56, 61, 65–66, 70

Writing:

- Writing samples for portfolios

Informal Assessment:

- **Diagnostic Checks**, pp. T23, T33, T43, T51, T86, T97, T105, T131, T147, T155

Theme Skills Test

End-of-Theme Assessment

Theme Skills Test:

- Assesses children's mastery of specific reading and language arts skills taught in the theme.

Kindergarten Benchmarks

For your planning, listed here are the instructional goals and activities that help develop benchmark behaviors for kindergartners. Use this list to plan instruction and to monitor children's progress. See the Checklist of skills found on p. T159.

Theme Lessons and Activities:	Benchmark Behaviors:
Oral Language • songs, rhymes, chants, finger plays • shared reading	• can listen to a story attentively • can participate in the shared reading experience
Phonemic Awareness • beginning sounds • syllables in spoken words	• can blend sounds into meaningful units
Phonics • initial consonants *s, m, r*	• can name single letters and their sounds • can decode some common CVC words
Concepts of Print • capital at the beginning of sentence • end punctuation (period, question mark)	• can recognize common print conventions
Reading • wordless stories • high-frequency words *I, see*	• can read and write a few words • can select a letter to represent a sound
Comprehension • sequence of events • inferences: making predictions	• can think critically about a text • can use effective reading strategies
Writing and Language • drawing and labeling images • using color words	• can label pictures using phonetic spellings • can write independently

Launching the Theme
Colors All Around

Theme Poster: Colors All Around

....

▶ Using the Theme Poster

Read the title of the poster. Tell children that they can see colors everywhere. Point to the fall scene and ask, **What colors do you see in this picture?** Continue with the pictures for winter, spring, and summer.

- Hang the poster in the classroom and have children point to and name different colors during opening routines or during transition times.
- Use the poster throughout the theme as a springboard for color activities.

Week 1 Children can look at the poster to see if they can find the colors of the shoes, lunchboxes, and pencils from *I Need a Lunchbox.*

Week 2 After reading In the *Big Blue Sea,* have children tell which color of fish they liked the best, and why.

Week 3 After rereading *I Went Walking,* have small groups talk about nature walks they have taken and the colorful animals that they saw along the way.

Multi-age Classroom

Related Themes

Grade 1 . . . Let's Look Around

Grade K . . . Colors All Around

▶ Theme Poem: "I Love Colors"

Read the poem aloud. Ask, *What do you notice about some of the words in the poem?* Point out that the color words are printed in the color of the word names.

Read the poem again, then have children echo-read. After several readings, name a color word and have a volunteer point to the correct word.

On-Going Project

> **Materials** • 18" x 24" sheets of oaktag • markers

Color Big Book Invite children to write and illustrate a class big book titled *I See.* Divide the class into small groups, and have each group select a color. Then each group brainstorms a list of things that are the color they selected. On different pieces of oaktag the groups draw pictures of the items they listed. As the children work, circulate to help them write the words *I see* and the name of the group's color on each page. They may also want to write other labels. When the children are finished, staple the book together and read it as a class. If you place the book in your Book Center, children can read it on their own. Another kindergarten class also may enjoying visiting your class to read the book. Make sure the children also show the book to their families and friends.

Higglety Pigglety: A Book of Rhymes, **page 10**

www.eduplace.com
Log onto *Education Place* for more activities relating to *Colors All Around.*

Lesson Planner CD-ROM
Customize your planning for *Colors All Around* with the Lesson Planner.

Book Adventure
www.bookadventure.org
This Internet reading-incentive program provides thousands of titles for students to read.

Home Connection

Send home the theme letter for *Colors All Around* to introduce the theme and suggest home activities (**Blackline Masters 27–28**).

For other suggestions relating to *Colors All Around* see **Home/Community Connections.**

Classroom Routines
Colors All Around

To introduce a routine...

1 Demonstrate the routine for the class.

2 Cycle every child through the routine at least once with supervision.

3 Establish ground rules for acceptable work products.

4 Check children's work.

5 Praise children's growing independence.

Instructional Routines
Same Sound Sort

Tell children to listen carefully as you say two words. If both words have the same beginning sound, children should raise their hands. If the words do not begin with the same sound, children should cover their ears. As you say the sounds, stretch out the initial sound. Ask, *Listen as I say two words: sssix, sssoap. Do you hear the same sound at the beginning of each word?*

Use words that practice the initial consonant of the week.

Phonics Center

Show children how to sort Picture Cards by beginning sounds. On Day 1, Alphafriend *Sammy Seal* will be in the Phonics Center, without the letter. Children sort pictures according to whether the beginning sound is /s/ or not /s/. On Day 2, children can make the connection between the letter  and the sound it stands for. By the end of the theme, children will sort Picture Cards according to the three letters of the theme: *m, r,* and *s.*

Word Wall

Introduce the Word Wall during this theme. Throughout the year you will place high-frequency words that the children learn on the Word Wall. Starting in Theme 4, word family words can be added in a different color. When children need to remember how to write a word they have learned, they can refer to the Word Wall.

Management Routines
Transition Time

When it is time to move to another activity or to line up, call out different colors of clothing. Children will have to listen carefully to know when they can proceed to the next activity. "If you have on purple, you may line up." or "Everyone wearing blue may get your snack.

Teacher's Note

Writing the letters of the alphabet on colored index cards provides an easy way to label the Word Wall sections. If you keep a basket filled with blank index cards and markers near your group meeting area, you will have the supplies easily accessible when you write new words to add to the wall.

Literature for Week 1

Different texts for different purposes

Teacher Read Aloud

Purposes

- oral language
- listening strategy
- comprehension skill

 Awards

- ⭐ Best Books for Children
- ⭐ Bank Street College Best Children's Books of the Year

Big Books:

Higglety Pigglety: A Book of Rhymes

Purposes:

- oral language development
- phonemic awareness

From Apples to Zebras: A Book of ABC's

Purposes

- alphabet recognition
- letters and sounds

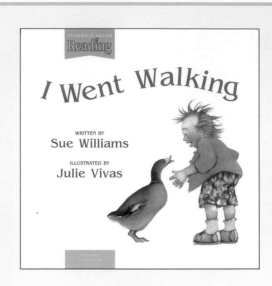

Big Book: **Main Selection**

Purposes

- concepts of print
- reading strategy
- story language
- comprehension skills

 Awards

- ⭐ American Bookseller Pick of the Lists
- ⭐ ALA Notable Children's Book
- ⭐ Best Books for Children
- ⭐ Oppenheim Toy Portfolio Best Book Award
- ⭐ Children's Book-of-the-Month Club Main Selection

Also available in Little Big Book and audiotape

Leveled Books

Also in the Big Book:
– Science Link

Purposes

- reading strategies
- comprehension skills
- concepts of print

Also available in Take-Home version

Purpose

- applying phonics skills and high-frequency words

On My Way Paperback

Beautiful Butterflies
by Demaris Tyler
page T153

Little Readers for Guided Reading
Collection K

Houghton Mifflin Classroom Bookshelf
Level K

Technology

www.eduplace.com

Log on to *Education Place* for more activities relating to *Colors All Around*.

www.bookadventure.org

This free Internet reading incentive program provides thousands of titles for students to read.

Suggested Daily Routines

Instructional Goals

Learning to Read

✓ *Phonemic Awareness:* Beginning Sounds, Syllables in Spoken Words

Strategy Focus: Predict/Infer

✓ *Comprehension Skill:* Sequence of Events

✓ *Phonics Skills*

Phonemic Awareness: Beginning Sound /s/

Initial Consonant S, s

Compare and Review: Initial Consonant: s

✓ *High-Frequency Word:* I

✓ *Concepts of Print:* Capitalize First Word in Sentence: End Punctuation

Word Work

Exploring Words: Color Words

Writing & Language

Vocabulary Skill: Using Describing Words

Writing Skill: Writing a Description

✓ = tested skills

Leveled Books

Have children read in appropriate levels daily.

Phonics Library
On My Way Practice Readers
Little Big Books
Houghton Mifflin Classroom Bookshelf

Day 1

Opening Routines, *T8–T9*

Word | Wall

• **Phonemic Awareness:** Beginning Sounds, Syllables in Spoken Words

Teacher Read Aloud
I Need a Lunch Box, T10–T11
• **Strategy:** Predict/Infer
• **Comprehension:** Sequence of Events

Phonics

Instruction
• Phonemic Awareness, Beginning Sound /s/, *T12–T13; Practice Book, 47–48*

Exploring Words
• Color Words, *T14*

Oral Language
• Using Describing Words, *T15*

Managing Small Groups
Teacher-Led Group
• Reread familiar **Phonics Library** selections

Independent Groups
• Finish *Practice Book, 45–48*
• *Phonics Center:* Theme 2, Week 1, Day 1
• Book, Writing, other Centers

Day 2

Opening Routines, *T16–T17*

Word | Wall

• **Phonemic Awareness:** Beginning Sounds, Syllables in Spoken Words

Sharing the Big Book
I Went Walking, T18–T19
• **Strategy:** Predict/Infer
• **Comprehension:** Sequence of Events

Phonics

Instruction, Practice
• Initial Consonant s, *T20–T21*
• *Practice Book, 49*

High Frequency Word
• New Word: *I, T22–T23*
• *Practice Book, 50*

Exploring Words
• Color Words, *T24*

Vocabulary Expansion
• Using Describing Words, *T25*

Managing Small Groups
Teacher-Led Group
• Begin *Practice Book, 49–50* and handwriting Blackline Masters 175 or 201.

Independent Groups
• Finish *Practice Book, 49–50* and handwriting Blackline Masters 175 or 201.
• *Phonics Center:* Theme 2, Week 1, Day 2
• Science, Art, other Centers

Technology

Lesson Planner CD-ROM: Customize your planning for *Colors All Around* with the Lesson Planner.

Day 3

Opening Routines, *T26–T27*

Word Wall

- **Phonemic Awareness:** Beginning Sounds, Syllables in Spoken Words

Sharing the Big Book
I Went Walking, T28–T31
- **Strategy:** Predict/Infer
- **Comprehension:** Sequence of Events, *T29; Practice Book,* 51
- **Concepts of Print:** Capitalize First Word in Sentence; End Punctuation, *T30*

Phonics

Practice, Application
- Initial Consonant *s, T34–T35*
Instruction
- Beginning Letter *s, T34–T35*
- **Phonics Library:** "My Red Boat," *T35*

Exploring Words
- Color Words, *T36*

✎ **Shared Writing**
- Writing a Description, *T37*
- Viewing and Speaking, *T37*

Managing Small Groups
Teacher-Led Group
- Read **Phonics Library** selection "My Red Boat"
- Begin *Practice Book,* 51

Independent Groups
- Finish *Practice Book,* 51
- Art, other Centers

Day 4

Opening Routines, *T38–T39*

Word Wall

- **Phonemic Awareness:** Beginning Sounds, Syllables in Spoken Words

Sharing the Big Book
Science Link: "What's My Favorite Color?," *T40–T41*
- **Strategy:** Predict/Infer
- **Comprehension:** Sequence of Events
- **Concepts of Print:** Capitalize First Word in Sentence; End Punctuation

Phonics

Practice
- Review Initial Consonant *s, T42–T43; Practice Book,* 52

Exploring Words
- Color Words, *T44*

✎ **Interactive Writing**
- Writing a Description, *T45*
- Viewing and Speaking, *T45*

Managing Small Groups
Teacher-Led Group
- Reread **Phonics Library** selection "My Red Boat"
- Begin *Practice Book,* 52

Independent Groups
- Finish *Practice Book,* 52
- *Phonics Center:* Theme 2, Week 1, Day 4
- Writing, other Centers

Day 5

Opening Routines, *T46–T47*

Word Wall

- **Phonemic Awareness:** Beginning Sounds, Syllables in Spoken Words

Revisiting the Literature
Comprehension: Sequence of Events, *T48*

Building Fluency
- **Phonics Library:** "My Red Boat," *T49*

Phonics

Review
- Initial Consonant *s, T50*

High-Frequency Word Review
- Word: *I, T51; Practice Book,* 53

Exploring Words
- Color Words, *T52*

✎ **Independent Writing**
- Journals: Favorite Color, *T53*

Managing Small Groups
- Reread familiar **Phonics Library** selections
- Begin *Practice Book,* 53, Blackline Master 36.

Independent Groups
- Reread **Phonics Library** selections
- Finish *Practice Book,* 53, Blackline Master 36.
- Centers

Setting up the Centers

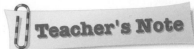

Management Tip Children mix together different colors of paint in this week's Art Center activity. It may be helpful to have a volunteer in the classroom to help out with this activity.

Phonics Center

Materials • Phonics Center materials for Theme 2, Week 1

Pairs work together to sort Picture Cards by initial sound. Cut the letter grids apart and put them into plastic bags, according to color. Put out the Workmats and open the Direction Chart to the appropriate day. See pages T13, T21, and T43 for this week's Phonics Center activities.

Book Center

Materials • color picture books

Children explore color as they browse through picture books. Fill your Center with books such as *Brown Bear, Brown Bear, What Do You See?* by Bill Martin, Jr., *Kente Colors* by Debbie Chocolate, and *Mouse Paint* by Ellen Stoll Walsh. See page T11 for this week's Book Center activity.

Writing Center

Materials • drawing paper • Blackline Master 34

Children create their own books about color. They draw illustrations and label them with color words. Children also write color words and draw a picture to complete **Blackline Master 34.** See pages T15 and T45 for this week's Writing Center activities.

I went walking.
What did you see?
I saw a red sign.

Science Center

Materials • picture books of farm animals • drawing paper • crayons

Children work in groups as they browse through the books and make a picture list of the animals they see. See page T19 for this week's Science Center activity.

Art Center

Materials • Blackline Master 35 • cups of red, blue, and yellow paint • paint brushes

Small groups work together to record what happens when they mix different colors of paint. See page T33 for this week's Art Center activity.

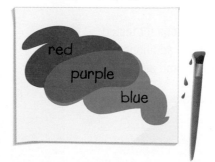

red
purple
blue

Day 1

Day at a Glance

Learning to Read

Teacher Read Aloud:

I Need a Lunch Box

☑ Learning About /s/, page T12

Word Work

Exploring Words, *page 14*

Writing & Language

Oral Language, *page T15*

 Half-Day Kindergarten

☑ Indicates lessons for tested skills. Choose additional activities as time allows.

Opening

Calendar

Sunday	Monday	Tuesday	Wednesday	Thursday	Friday	Saturday
			1	2	3	4
5	6	7	8	9	10	11
12	13	14	15	16	17	18
19	20	21	22	23	24	25
26	27	28	29	30	31	

Conduct your calendar routine, having children repeat the names of the days of the week after you. Call on volunteers to name different colors on the calendar.

Daily Message

Modeled Writing Celebrate starting a new reading theme by including the theme title in your daily message. Discuss with children the colors they see around them.

> Today we start a new theme called Colors All Around. Brian has a new green sweater today.

Daily Phonemic Awareness
Beginning Sounds

- *Listen* sssix, sssoap. *Say the words with me:* six, soap. *Do you hear the same sound at the beginning of each word? ...So do I.* Six *and* soap *begin with the same sound.*

- Tell children that they will play Same Sound Sort. *If the words begin with the same sound, raise your hands. If the words do not begin with the same sound, cover your ears.*

bike/bell	cat/dog
milk/mouse	rock/room
sock/sun	ten/top
nest/nose	sink/mop

Syllables in Spoken Words

- Tell children that they will listen for the word parts in their names. Choose a child with a two-syllable name and say their name aloud: *Sandy.* Say *Sandy* again, clapping the syllables. *How many claps did you hear? ...Yes, two! Now say and clap the name with me:* San-dy.

- Continue with other two-syllable names.

Getting Ready to Learn

To help plan their day, tell children that they will

- listen to a story called *I Need a Lunch Box.*

- meet an Alphafriend, Sammy Seal.

- learn more about colors and color words in the Book Center.

Day 1

Purposes • oral language • listening strategy
• comprehension skill

Selection Summary

A young boy is envious when his older sister gets a new lunch box for school. His fascination with lunch boxes grows until, on the first day of school, his father surprises him with a lunch box.

Key Concepts

Colors
Days of the week
Needs and wants

English Language Learners

Before you read, review or introduce colors and the days of the week.

Teacher Read Aloud

Oral Language/Comprehension

▶ **Building Background**

If you have one, show a lunch box or an insulated lunch bag. Talk about what it is used for, how it is packed, and what children like or don't like about it.

Strategy: Predict/Infer

Display *I Need a Lunch Box*. Read aloud the names of the author and illustrator. Allow children to comment on the title and the cover illustration.

Teacher Modeling Model the strategy for predicting what a book will be about.

Think Aloud

How can I tell what I Need a Lunch Box is about?

• *I can look at the cover. Maybe this is the boy who needs a lunch box.*

• *I wonder why the boy needs a lunch box. Maybe he's going to school. What do you think? Let's read to find out.*

Comprehension Focus: Sequence of Events

Teacher Modeling Tell children that things in a story happen in a certain order.

Think Aloud

It's important to think about the order as you read. I'll pay attention to what happens first, next, and last in the story. You can help me do that. Listen as I read.

▶ Listening to the Story

As you read, help children imagine that the boy is actually telling the story.

▶ Responding

Summarizing the Story Help children summarize parts of the story.

- *Did the boy really need a lunch box? Why do you think he wanted one? Did you ever want something you didn't really need?*

- *What did Doris get to take to school? Why didn't the boy get these things? How did he feel about that?*

- *Why do you think the boy dreamed of lunch boxes? What colors did he dream about?*

- *How does the story end? Were we right when we predicted the boy needed a lunch box for school?*

Practice Book pages 45–46 Children will complete the pages during small group time.

Practice Book p. 46

Name

Practice Book p. 45

Name

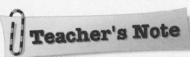

Teacher's Note

Create a chart in the Writing Center for the basic color words: *blue, green, yellow, orange, red, purple, brown, black,* and *white.* For each color, use that color crayon or marker to write the color word. Add to the chart as children suggest other color words.

At Group Time

Book Center

Have a rainbow of color books available in the Book Center. Include favorites like *Brown Bear, Brown Bear, What Do You See?* by Bill Martin, Jr. and *Freight Train* by Donald Crews. Other good choices for exploring colors include *Planting a Rainbow* by Lois Ehlert, *Kente Colors* by Debbi Chocolate, *Mouse Paint* by Ellen Stoll Walsh, and *Animals Black and White* by Phyllis Limbacher Tildes.

Home Connection

A take-home version of Sammy Seal's Song is on an **Alphafriends Blackline Master.** Children can share the song with their families.

English Language Learners

Children may confuse the /s/ and /z/ sounds. Display Picture Cards for *s* and ask children to repeat the names aloud. Make sure children know the *s* words in Sammy Seal's song: *seal, sea, sail, seagull, salute.*

Phonemic Awareness
✔️ Beginning Sound

▶ Introducing the Alphafriend: Sammy Seal

Follow the Alphafriend routine to introduce the first Alphafriend, Sammy Seal. Tell children that Alphafriends will help them remember important sounds. Start with a riddle.

1 **Alphafriend Riddle** Read these clues:

- *Our Alphafriend's sound is /s/. Say it with me: /s/.*
- *This animal ssswims and dives in the sssea all day long.*
- *He has flippers instead of hands and feet, but he barks like a dog.*
- *You might sssee him balance a ball at the aquarium or the zoo.*

When most hands are up, call on children until they guess *seal*.

2 **Pocket Chart** Display Sammy Seal in the pocket chart. Say his name, stretching the /s/ sound slightly, and have children echo this.

3 📼 **Alphafriend Audiotape** Play Sammy Seal's song. Listen for /s/ words in Sammy's song.

4 **Alphafolder** Have children look at the scene and name all the /s/ pictures.

5 **Summarize**

- *What is our Alphafriend's name? What is his sound?*
- *What words in our Alphafriend's song start with /s/?*
- *Each time you look at Sammy Seal this week, remember the /s/ sound.*

Sammy Seal's Song

(Tune: "Yankee Doodle")

Sammy Seal will sail the sea
when summer is the season.
Sammy Seal will sail the sea
and never need a reason.
Sammy Seal will sail the sea
in very sunny weather.
Sammy Seal salutes a seagull
as they sail together!

▶ Listening for / s /

Compare Display Sammy Seal. Tell children you'll name some pictures, and they should signal "thumbs up" for each one that begins like Sammy's name. Volunteers put the card below Sammy's picture. If the picture doesn't begin like *Sammy*, children should signal "thumbs down," and leave the card in the bottom row.

Pictures: *sandwich, man, ten, six, rock, sun, boat, sandbox.*

Tell children they will sort more pictures in the Phonics Center today.

▶ Apply

Practice Book pages 47–48 Children will complete the pages at small group time.

At Group Time

Phonics Center

Use the Phonics Center materials for **Theme 2, Week 1, Day 1**.

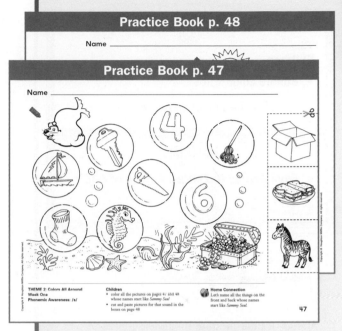

Practice Book p. 48

Name _____

Practice Book p. 47

Name _____

THEME 2: Colors All Around
Week One
Phonemic Awareness: /s/

Children
• color all the pictures on pages 47 and 48 whose names start like *Sammy Seal*
• cut and paste pictures for that sound in the boxes on page 48

Home Connection
Let's name all the things on the front and back whose names start like *Sammy Seal*.

47

Day 1

Exploring Words

▶ Color Words

- Display *From Apples to Zebras: A Book of ABC's*, page 29. **What do you see? That's right, colors. Name them with me.** Point to each color and name it with children. Check to see how aware of color words children seem to be.

- Now tell children to watch as you point to the color words. Explain that each color has a word that you can read.

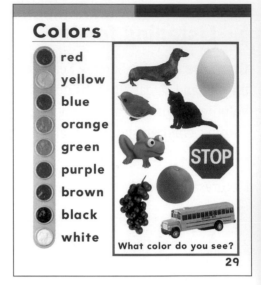

Colors

red
yellow
blue
orange
green
purple
brown
black
white

What color do you see?

29

From Apples to Zebras: A Book of ABC's,
page 29

Writing Opportunity Have each child choose a color square to represent a favorite color. Then ask each child to write his or her name on the square and, if they choose, copy the color word. Next, help children create a graph of their favorite colors. Discuss the completed graph with questions. such as: *How many children like blue? How many children like green? Which color is liked by the most children?*

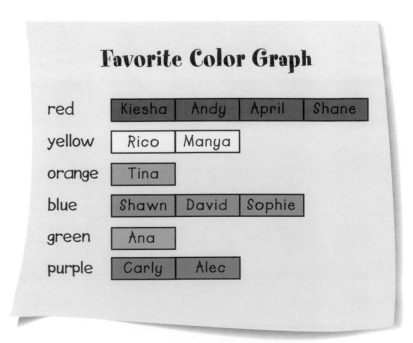

Favorite Color Graph

red	Kiesha	Andy	April	Shane
yellow	Rico	Manya		
orange	Tina			
blue	Shawn	David	Sophie	
green	Ana			
purple	Carly	Alec		

OBJECTIVES

Children
- explore color words
- create a class color graph

MATERIALS

- *From Apples to Zebras: A Book of ABC's,* page 29

Teacher's Note

Ahead of time prepare multiple squares of colored construction paper. The colors should match those in "Colors," on page 29 in *From Apples to Zebras: A Book of ABC's.* Children will need the squares to complete the color graph.

Oral Language

▶ Using Describing Words

- Read aloud "I Love Colors," page 10 of *Higglety Pigglety: A Book of Rhymes*.

- Read the poem again, asking children to listen for the color words.

- Then have children place the picture and color word cards in a pocket chart as you point to and read each color word in the poem.

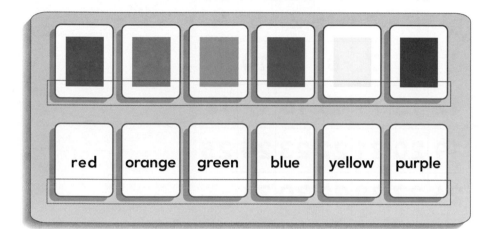

| red | orange | green | blue | yellow | purple |

At Group Time
Writing Center

Materials • drawing paper • crayons or markers

Hang the pocket chart in the Writing Center. Have children make color books by drawing pictures to illustrate different colors. They can refer to the Word Cards to help them label each page with a color word.

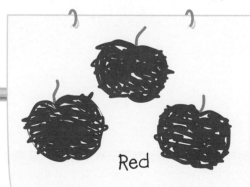

Red

📎 Teacher's Note

Children enjoy making books using pages of different sizes. Stock your Writing Center with paper cut into 6-inch squares for this book-making activity.

📁 Portfolio Opportunity

Save children's color books as examples of beginning-of-the-year drawing and writing work.

👤 English Language Learners

Have children write each color word in the appropriate color.

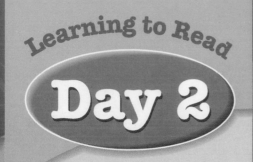

Day at a Glance

Learning to Read

Big Book:

I Went Walking

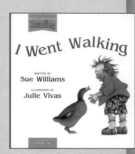

I Went Walking

WRITTEN BY
Sue Williams

ILLUSTRATED BY
Julie Vivas

- ☑ **Phonics: Initial Consonant s,** *page T20*

- ☑ **High-Frequency Word: I,** *page T21*

Word Work

Exploring Words, *page T24*

Writing & Language

Vocabulary Expansion, *page T25*

 Half-Day Kindergarten

☑ Indicates lessons for tested skills. Choose additional activities as time allows.

Opening

Calendar

Sunday	Monday	Tuesday	Wednesday	Thursday	Friday	Saturday
			1	2	3	4
5	6	7	8	9	10	11
12	13	14	15	16	17	18
19	20	21	22	23	24	25
26	27	28	29	30	31	

Choose a color for each day of the week. Have children wear or bring in something of that color to celebrate the day.

Daily Message

Modeled Writing As you write the daily message, describe what you are doing. *The first word I want to write is* today. *Today is also the first word in my sentence so I will begin it with a capital letter.*

Today we have art at 10:00. What colors will we mix?

Daily Phonemic Awareness
Beginning Sounds

- Have children name the pictures.

- Hold up and name Picture Card *bat*. **Say the word with me.**

- *Look for a picture that starts with the same sound as* bat. *Is it* jeep? *Is it* rake? *Is it* bike? *Yes, it's* bike. *Say the two words together.*

Syllables in Spoken Words

- Play a clapping game with children's names. *I'll say a name. Clap it with me.* Lily. *Listen.* Li-ly. *How many claps? Right. Two. Now it's your turn.* Ben-ja-min. *Yes, three claps.*

- Continue until you have clapped several children's names.

Getting Ready to Learn

To help plan their day, tell children that they will

- listen to a Big Book: *I Went Walking*.

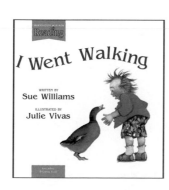

- learn the new letters *S* and *s*, and see words that begin with *s*.

- list farm animals in the Science Center.

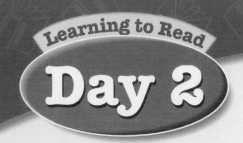

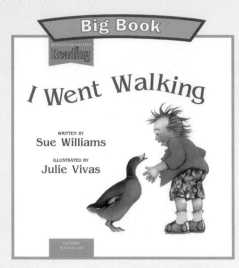

HOUGHTON MIFFLIN
Reading

I Went Walking

WRITTEN BY
Sue Williams

ILLUSTRATED BY
Julie Vivas

Purposes • concepts of print • story language
• reading strategy • comprehension skill

Selection Summary
While talking a walk, a young boy has farm animals of different colors join him.

Key Concepts
Color words
Animal names

English Language Learners

Help children with the sentence *I went walking*, explaining it as: *I went for a walk.* For the clause *looking at me*, restate the phrase as two simple sentences: *I saw a (animal name). The (animal name) was looking at me.*

Sharing the Big Book
Oral Language/Comprehension

▶ Building Background

Ask children to remember a walk you've taken together as a class or one they've taken to or from school. Have them tell all the things they saw on the walk. Then introduce the book *I Went Walking* by Sue Williams. Tell children that this book is about a walk, too.

Strategy: Predict/Infer

Teacher Modeling Model how to predict what the book will be about by previewing the title and the pictures.

Think Aloud

Before I read, I can use clues from the title of the story and the pictures to predict what a book is about.

• *The title says I Went Walking and shows a picture of a boy. When I look at the first few pages, I see that the boy is walking. I also see that a cat has joined him.*

• *Maybe the boy sees other animals on his walk. Let's read the book and see what happens.*

✓ Comprehension Focus: Sequence of Events

Teacher Modeling Remind children that good readers think about the order in which things happen in a story.

Think Aloud

As I read, I'll think about what happens first, next, and last. This will help me remember the story.

▶ Sharing the Story

As you read aloud, emphasize the story sequence with words like *first, then,* and *next.* Help children discover the next animal by using the picture clues.

▶ Responding

Personal Response Encourage children to use color words as they respond.

- *Did you like the story? What was your favorite part?*

- *Who can name the animals the boy saw? Use the pictures to help you remember.*

- *Did the boy have fun on the walk? How can you tell?*

Literature Circle Have children name their favorite animal in the story. Ask them to share titles of other books they may have read about farm animals.

At Group Time

Science Center

Materials • picture books of farm animals • drawing paper • crayons

Place several picture books about farm animals in the Science Center. Have children work in groups of two or three to explore the books and create a picture list of farm animals. Children can refer to the Big Book text and in the picture books to label and draw their lists.

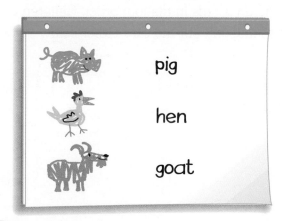

pig

hen

goat

Extra Support

Before reading, some children may need a more detailed picture walk to identify each animal.

OBJECTIVES

Children

- identify words that begin with /s/
- identify pictures whose names start with the letter s
- form the letters S, s

MATERIALS

- **Alphafriend Card** Sammy Seal
- **Letter Card** s
- **Picture Cards** six, sun, sandbox, mat, mop, toast, ten
- **Blackline Master 175**
- **Phonics Center:** Theme 2, Week 1, Day 2

Extra Support

To help children remember the sound for s, point out that the letter's name gives a clue to its sound: s, /s/.

Phonics

✓ Initial Consonant s

▶ Develop Phonemic Awareness

Beginning Sound Read the lyrics to Sammy Seal's song and have children echo it line-for-line. Have them listen for the /s/ words and "sit" up each time they hear one.

> ### Sammy Seal's Song
> (Tune: "Yankee Doodle")
>
> Sammy Seal will sail the sea
>   when summer is the season.
> Sammy Seal will sail the sea
>   and never need a reason.
> Sammy Seal will sail the sea
>   in very sunny weather.
> Sammy Seal salutes a seagull
>   as they sail together!

▶ Connect Sounds to Letters

Beginning Letter Display the *Sammy Seal* card, and point out the letter on the picture. *This time, Sammy has a letter. What is it? The letter* s *stands for the sound /s/, as in* ssseal. *When you see an* s, *remember* Sammy Seal. *That will help you remember the sound /s/.*

Write *seal* on the board. Underline the *s. What is the first letter in the word* seal? (s) **Seal** *starts with /s/, so* s *is the first letter I write for* seal.

Compare In a pocket chart, display the *Sammy Seal* card along with Letter Card *s.* Place the Picture Cards in random order. Children can name a picture, say the beginning sound, and put the card either below the *s* or to the side of the pocket chart.

Tell children they will sort more pictures in the Phonics Center today.

▶ Handwriting

Writing S, s Tell children that now they'll learn to write the letters that stand for /s/: capital *S* and small *s*. Write each letter as you recite the handwriting rhyme. Children can chant each rhyme as they "write" the letter in the air.

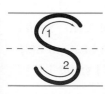

Handwriting Rhyme: S

S looks like a snake, curve left then right. From top to bottom, makes it right.

Handwriting Rhyme: s

Small *s* looks like a snake, too. Curve left then right, that's all you do.

▶ Apply

Practice Book page 49 Children will complete this page at small group time.

Blackline Master 175 This page provides additional handwriting practice.

At Group Time

Use the Phonics Center materials for **Theme 2, Week 1, Day 2**.

Practice Book p. 49

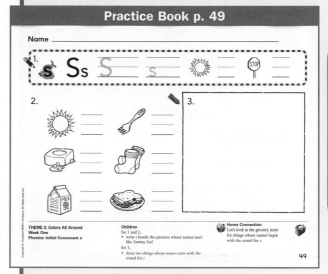

Name _____

THEME 2: Colors All Around
Week One
Phonics: Initial Consonant *s*

Children
for 1 and 2,
• write *s* beside the pictures whose names start like *Sammy Seal*
for 3,
• draw two things whose names start with the sound for *s*

Home Connection
Let's look at the grocery store for things whose names begin with the sound for *s*.

49

📎 Teacher's Note

Handwriting practice for the continuous stroke style is available on **Blackline Master 201**.

Portfolio Opportunity

Save the Practice Book page to show children's grasp of the letter-sound association.

Save **Blackline Master 175** for a handwriting sample.

OBJECTIVES

Children

• read and write the high-frequency word *I*

MATERIALS

• **Word Card** *I*

• **Picture Cards** *cut, hop, run*

• **Punctuation Card:** period

• ***Higglety Pigglety: A Book of Rhymes***, page 10

✓ High-Frequency Word

New Word: I

▶ Teach

Tell children that today they will learn to read and write a word. Explain that it's a very important word to know because you use it to tell about yourself. Say *I* and use it in context.

    I drink milk.   *I* like cats.   *I* like to sing.

Write *I* on the board. Point out that it's a letter as well as a word. Ask children to name the letter. Explain that the word *I* always uses the capital form. **Spell I with me, capital I.** Then lead children in a chant, clapping on each beat, to help them remember that *I* is spelled *capital I*: **capital I spells I, capital I spells I.**

Word Wall Introduce the Word Wall. Explain that this is where you will put words children will learn to read and write. Post *I*, and ask children to tell why you put it where you did. Tell children to check the Word Wall if they need to remember how to write the word *I*.

▶ Practice

Reading Tell children that they can use this new word to tell about themselves. *I'll use some pictures and the new word* I. *You help me read.*

In a pocket chart, build rebus sentences. Add the end punctuation and tell children that it marks the end of a sentence.

Display **Higglety Pigglety: A Book of Rhymes,** page 10.

- Share the poem "I Love Colors" aloud.

- Reread the title of the poem. *I'll read the title again. This time I'll read it slowly. You listen for the word* I. *When you hear it, raise your hand.*

- Call on children to point to the word *I* each time it appears in the poem.

Higglety Pigglety: A Book of Rhymes, page 10

▶ **Apply**

Practice Book page 50 Children will read and write *I* as they complete the Practice Book page.

Practice Book p. 50

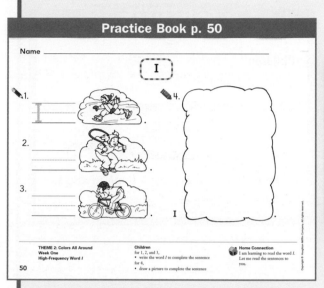

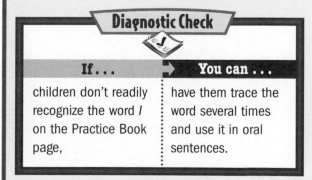

If...	You can...
children don't readily recognize the word *I* on the Practice Book page,	have them trace the word several times and use it in oral sentences.

High-Frequency Word (T23)

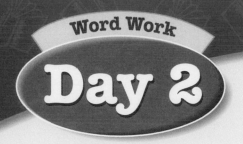

Day 2

OBJECTIVES

Children
- discuss color words

MATERIALS

- **Big Book:** *I Went Walking*
- ***From Apples to Zebras: A Book of ABC's,*** page 29

Exploring Words

▶ **Color Words**

Reread a few pages of the Big Book, *I Went Walking*. Focus on the color words in an oral context.

■ *Listen:* **I saw a red cow looking at me.** *What word tells the color? What else is red?* (sample answer: bird) *Who can make a sentence just like this about a bird?* (I saw a red bird looking at me.)

■ Continue with each color mentioned in the book. Children who are able can make their own books based on the pattern of the text. You can record their ideas.

Writing Opportunity Have children draw pictures of something colorful. Children who are able can label their pictures with the color word. They can use page 29 of *From Apples to Zebras* as a reference.

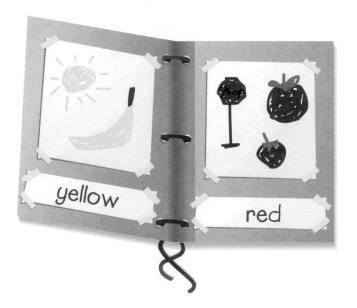

Vocabulary Expansion

▶ **Using Describing Words**

Talk about how in the story *I Went Walking,* the author wrote about colorful animals. Remind children that they can use color to describe things too.

Viewing and Speaking Page through the story, having children name the animals and their colors. Chart the responses.

■ For each animal, have children think of other colors that the animals might be. Encourage creative and fanciful descriptions, too.

■ List children's suggestions on the chart. Repeat for each animal, prompting children with questions as needed.

Animal	Color	More Color Words
cat	black	gray, black spotted, yellow striped
horse	brown	black, white, black spotted

■ Read the chart aloud. Congratulate children for their good thinking and for all the words they knew to add.

At Group Time

Art Center

Materials • drawing paper • crayons or markers

Have children draw pictures of animals they have seen in their neighborhoods. Children can label their drawings.

yellow

Day 3

Day at a Glance

Learning to Read

Big Book:

I Went Walking

 Phonics: Initial Consonant s, *page T34*

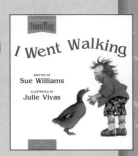

Reading

I Went Walking

WRITTEN BY
Sue Williams

ILLUSTRATED BY
Julie Vivas

Word Work

Exploring Words, *page T36*

Writing & Language

Shared Writing, *page T37*

☀ Half-Day Kindergarten

✓ Indicates lessons for tested skills. Choose additional activities as time allows.

Opening

Calendar

Sunday	Monday	Tuesday	Wednesday	Thursday	Friday	Saturday
			1	2	3	4
5	6	7	8	9	10	11
12	13	14	15	16	17	18
19	20	21	22	23	24	25
26	27	28	29	30	31	

As you complete your calendar routine, explore the color of the day. *Who wore something red today? Who brought in something red? Tell us about it.*

Daily Message

Modeled Writing Include colors and children's names into today's daily message. Children can write their own names or the first letter of their names.

Erica wore a red dress. Miguel and Silvia have red shirts. I have red socks!

Word Wall

Introduce the Word Wall routine. Ask children if they can find the word that they added to the Word Wall yesterday. Call on a volunteer to point it out. Have children chant the spelling of the word: *capital* **I** *spells* **I**.

Routines

···

✓ Daily Phonemic Awareness
Beginning Sounds

- *Let's listen for beginning sounds. I will say two words, you tell me which word begins with Sammy Seal's sound, /s/. Listen: five, six.*

- *Say the words with me: five, six. Which word begins with /s/?... Yes, six begins with /s/.*

- Continue with the words shown.

✓ Syllables in Spoken Words

- Play a clapping game with children's names. *I'll say a name. Clap it with me.* Jamal. *Listen.* Ja-mal. *How many claps? Right. Two. Now it's your turn.* Zo-e. *Yes, three claps.*

- Continue with other children's names.

sun/me
fish/seal
sock/mitten
soap/happy
rock/sand
north/see
dance/sing
sack/bag
sink/tub

Getting Ready to Learn

To help plan their day, tell children that they will

- reread and talk about the Big Book: *I Went Walking*.

- read a story called "My Red Boat."

- explore favorite colors in the Art Center.

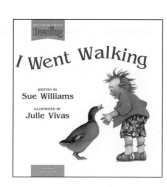

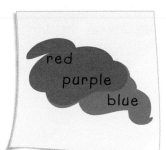

Sharing the Big Book

OBJECTIVES

Children

- identify sequence
- recognize use of capital letter at the beginning of a sentence
- recognize use of end punctuation

Big Book

Reading

I Went Walking

WRITTEN BY
Sue Williams

ILLUSTRATED BY
Julie Vivas

Reading for Understanding Reread the story, emphasizing color words. Pause for Supporting Comprehension points.

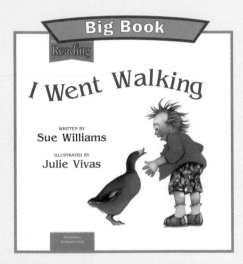

Extra Support

Provide additional practice with making predictions. Pause at each page for children to predict what animal the boy will see next.

I went walking.

What did you see?

2   3

pages 2–3

I saw a black cat looking at me.

4   5

pages 4–5

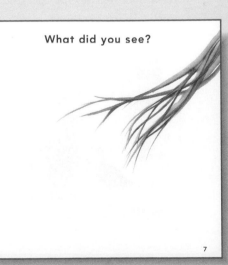

I went walking.

What did you see?

6   7

pages 6–7

I saw a brown horse
looking at me.

8

9

pages 8–9

I went walking.

What did you see?

10

11

pages 10–11

I saw a red cow
looking at me.

12

13

pages 12–13

▶ Supporting Comprehension

pages 2–3

Strategy: Predict/Infer

Teacher-Student Modeling Review how you made predictions yesterday before reading the book. Prompts:

■ *What did the book cover tell us about the story? Did we read about a boy taking a walk? Look at the pictures. How did you guess what the boy would see next?*

pages 4–5

Noting Details

■ *Were you right? How did you know the boy would see a cat?* (I can see part of the cat in the basket; the basket is now empty; the boy is hugging a black cat.)

pages 8–9

✓ Comprehension Focus: Sequence of Events

Teacher-Student Modeling Remind children that events in a story happen in a certain order. *This is a good story to figure out what happens next. Who can tell us what animal the boy will see next? I'll ask you to do that as I read.*

pages 10–11

Noting Details

■ *What does the boy have to climb to get on the cow?*

DAY 3

....

▶ Supporting Comprehension

page 14–15

Noting Details

■ *What animals has the boy seen so far?* (a black cat, a brown horse, a red cow)

pages 14–15

....

pages 18–19

Strategy: Predict/Infer

Student Modeling *What animal will the boy see next? How do you know?*

....

Revisiting the Text

pages 14–15

Concepts of Print

 Capitalize First Word in Sentence; End Punctuation

■ Frame the sentence on page 14. Remind children that the word *I* is always spelled with a capital letter. Tell children that the first word in a sentence also begins with a capital letter. Then point to the end of the sentence. *All sentences have end marks. We use a period at the end of a telling sentence. Who will find another period?*

pages 16–17

pages 18–19

pages 20–21

pages 22–23

pages 24–25

······························· Sharing the Big Book ·······························

▶ **Supporting Comprehension**

pages 20–21

Noting Details

■ *Is this the same animal you saw on page 19? How is it different?* (It is cleaner; the boy has washed off the mud.)

pages 24–25

Noting Details

■ *What does the dog do to show he is friendly? Would you like to have a dog like this? Why or why not?*

pages 24–25

☑ **Comprehension Focus: Sequence of Events**

Student Modeling *What will happen next? How do you know?*

DAY 3

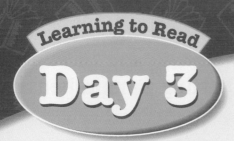

▶ ## Supporting Comprehension

pages 28–29

✓ **Comprehension Focus: Sequence of Events**

Student Modeling *How does the story end?*

 **Teacher's Note**

Language Patterns On a rereading, children can use the predictability of the text to chime in and increase their participation.

 Challenge

Some children will be able to read many words in the story. Others will "pretend read" by using the predictability of the text and the strong language pattern. Let these children read with partners.

I went walking.

What did you see?

pages 26–27

I saw a lot of animals following me!

pages 28–29

pages 30–31

▶ Responding to the Story

Retelling Use prompts to help children summarize the selection:

■ *What did the boy do at the beginning of the story?*

■ *What animals did the boy see during his walk?*

■ *How does knowing what will happen next help you to remember the story?*

■ *How was the ending different from the rest of the story?*

Practice Book page 51 Children will complete the page at small group time.

Literature Circle Have small groups discuss what might happen if the book were to continue. *What other animals might the boy see? What color would these animals be?*

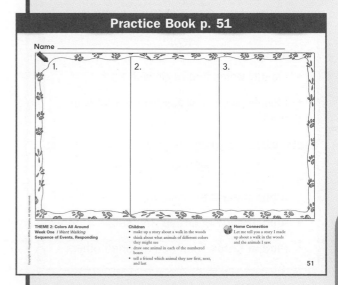

Practice Book p. 51

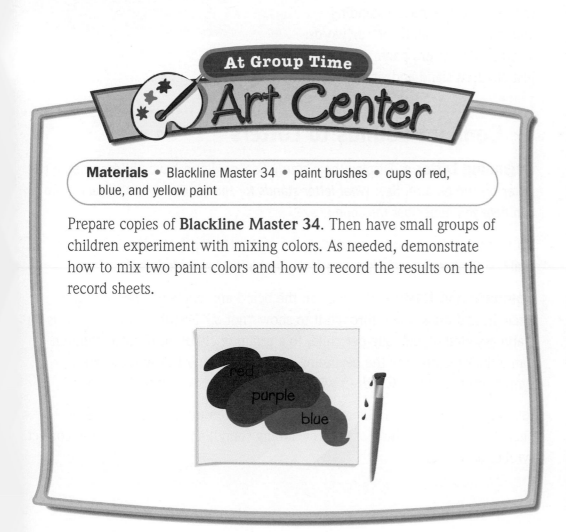

At Group Time

Art Center

Materials • Blackline Master 34 • paint brushes • cups of red, blue, and yellow paint

Prepare copies of **Blackline Master 34**. Then have small groups of children experiment with mixing colors. As needed, demonstrate how to mix two paint colors and how to record the results on the record sheets.

red
purple
blue

DAY 3

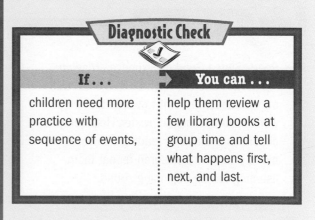

Diagnostic Check

If . . .	You can . . .
children need more practice with sequence of events,	help them review a few library books at group time and tell what happens first, next, and last.

Responding (T33)

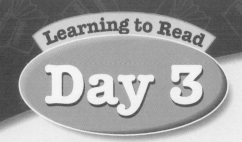
OBJECTIVES

Children

- identify words that begin with /s/
- identify pictures whose names start with the letter *s.*

MATERIALS

- **Alphafriend Card** *Sammy Seal*
- **Alphafriend Audiotape** Theme 2
- **Picture Cards** for s and assorted others

Extra Support

Read "Sing a Song of Sixpence," *Higglety Pigglety: A Book of Rhymes,* page 11. Call on volunteers to point to words that begin with /s/ in the tongue twister. Help verify children's choices by reading the words aloud and having children repeat them, listening for the beginning sound.

Phonics

✓ Initial Consonant s

▶ Develop Phonemic Awareness

Beginning Sound Read the lyrics to Sammy Seal's song aloud, and have children echo it line-for-line. Have them listen for the /s/ words.

Tell children that you will read the song again. *This time, if you hear a word that begins with /s/ stand up. If you hear another /s/ word, sit down. We'll stand up and sit down each time we hear an /s/ word. Let's practice with the first line.* As you say the first line, model standing and sitting alternately for /s/ words. Then say the entire poem, having just children stand and sit for /s/ words.

> ### Sammy Seal's Song
> (Tune: "Yankee Doodle")
>
> Sammy Seal will sail the sea
> when summer is the season.
> Sammy Seal will sail the sea
> and never need a reason.
> Sammy Seal will sail the sea
> in very sunny weather.
> Sammy Seal salutes a seagull
> as they sail together!

▶ Connect Sounds to Letters

Beginning Letter s Display the *Sammy Seal* card and have children name the letter on the picture. Say: *What letter stands for the sound /s/, as in* seal? *Who can help you remember the sound /s/?*

Write *seal* on the board, underlining the *s. What is the first letter in the word* seal? (s) Seal *starts with /s/, so s is the first letter I write for* seal.

Compare and Review Write *Ss* on the board and circle it. Then write *Ss,* circle it, and draw a line through it to show "not *s.*" Distribute Picture Cards for *s* and assorted others, one per child, to a group of children. In turn, children name their picture, say the beginning sound, and stand below the correct symbol on the board. Children without Picture Cards verify their decisions.

Repeat the activity with different groups of children until each child has a chance to name a picture, say the beginning sound, and stand below the correct symbol on the board.

Colors All Around

Applying Skills

▶ Introducing the Story

Let's look at the title page. It says "My Red Boat." What kind of boat could it be? Together identify pictures whose names start with /s/ on the title page.

Let's look at the pictures. That's a good way to tell what a story will be about. You tell me what you think it will be about.

As you do a picture walk, guide children in a discussion of the pictures.

▶ Coached Reading

Have children look carefully at each page before discussing it with you. Prompts:

page 1   *What kind of a boat is in this story?* (a sailboat) *What tells you that?*

page 4   *What color sail did the boy and his dad make?* (red)

page 5   *What is happening on this page?* (It is the big sailboat race.)

pages 6–7   *Which sailboat won the race? How do you know?*

Now let's go back and look at each page to find things that begin with Sammy Seal's sound, s-s-s.

Purposes

- read a wordless story
- find pictures beginning with /s/

My Red Boat
by Susan Gorman-Howe
illustrated by Lauren Scheuer

1

2   **3**

Race at 6:00

4   **5**

6   **7**

DAY 3

 Home Connection

Children can color the pictures in the take-home version of "My Red Boat." After rereading on Day 4, they can take it home to read to family members.

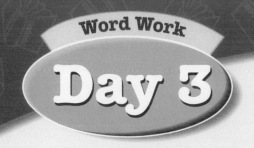

Day 3

Children
• explore color words

• *From Apples to Zebras: A Book of ABC's,* page 29

Exploring Words

▶ Color Words

Display page 29 of *From Apples to Zebras: A Book of ABC's.* Remind children that they have been talking about colors. Call on volunteers to point to and name the colors on the page.

■ Discuss with children how color words help them describe what something looks like. Then make a color chart for the Writing Center like the one on page 29 of *From Apples to Zebras.* Begin by listing the featured color words on the left side of the chart. If possible, use the appropriate color for each color word.

■ Have children brainstorm items for each color. Record their suggestions by drawing simple line drawings that children can then color in.

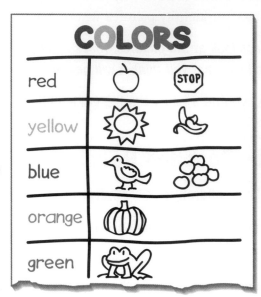

Writing Opportunity Have children create a Color Word Bank page in their journals. Children copy the words from the chart, then they draw objects for each specific color to complete their pages.

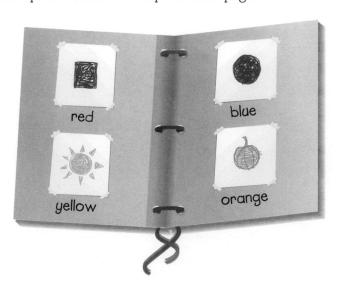

Shared Writing

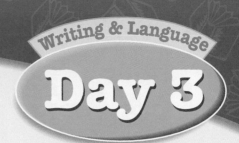
▶ Writing a Description

Viewing and Speaking Take a picture walk of *I Went Walking* and have children retell the story in their own words.

■ Tell children that they will write their own *I Went Walking* story. Take children on a brief walk around the school or the school grounds. As you walk, point out the colors of different objects.

■ When you return to the classroom, ask children to share their observations. Record all suggestions on chart paper.

DAY 3

English Language Learners

Invite children to create a "Book of New Words," where they can draw pictures of words they have learned during this theme. Help children add color or other describing words.

Day 4

Day at a Glance

Learning to Read

Big Book:

What's My Favorite Color?

✓ **Phonics:**
Review Initial
Consonant
/s/, page T42

Word Work

Exploring Words, *page T44*

Writing & Language

Interactive Writing, *page T45*

 Half-Day Kindergarten

✓ Indicates lessons for tested
skills. Choose additional
activities as time allows.

Opening

Calendar

Sunday	Monday	Tuesday	Wednesday	Thursday	Friday	Saturday
			1	2	3	4
5	6	7	8	9	10	11
12	13	14	15	16	17	18
19	20	21	22	23	24	25
26	27	28	29	30	31	

Talk about today's color as you complete the calendar routine. Encourage children to describe the colors they've worn. Be sure to share your own contribution too.

Daily Message

Modeled Writing Use some words that begin with *s* in today's message. Have volunteers circle each *s* at the beginning of a word.

Sal has on
brown socks
today.

Call on a volunteer to point out the word *I* on the Word Wall. Have children chant the spelling of the word: *capital* I *spells* I.

Routines

 Daily Phonemic Awareness
Beginning Sounds

- *Listen:* pig, pink. *Say the words with me:* pig, pink. *Do you hear the same sound at the beginning of each word? Yes,* pig *and* pink *begin with the same sound.* Help children isolate the beginning sound, / p /.

- Play Same Sound Sort. *I'll say two words. If they begin with the same sound, raise your hands. If they do not, cover your ears.* Help children isolate the beginning sound to verify their decisions.

duck/doll	rake/hat	bird/bat
cat/dog	leaf/lion	soap/sun

Syllables in Spoken Words

- *Today, we'll clap the word parts we hear in color words. Listen:* pur-ple.

- Say *purple* again, clapping the syllables. *How many claps did you hear?... Yes, two! Now say and clap the word with me:* pur-ple.

- Continue with other color words.

Getting Ready to Learn

To help plan their day, tell children that they will

- read the Science Link: *What's My Favorite Color?*

- sort pictures in the Phonics Center.

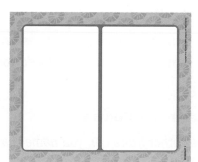

- reread a story called "My Red Boat."

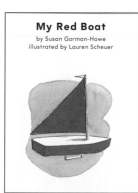

OBJECTIVES

Children

- identify sequence

- recognize use of capital letter at the beginning of a sentence

- recognize use of end punctuation: period, question mark

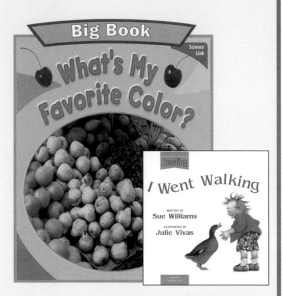

Big Book

pages 33-38

English Language Learners

Before working with the selection, review or introduce fruit names. Then have children classify fruits according to color, taste, or shape.

Sharing the Big Book

Science Link

▶ **Building Background**

Ask children to name their favorite fruit. Read aloud the title of the selection and discuss the photograph. Invite children to name the fruits and describe their colors.

Reading for Understanding Pause for discussion as you share the selection.

pages 34–35

Strategy: Predict/Infer

Student Modeling Point out to children that the title asks a question, *What's My Favorite Color?*, and that the selection shows different kinds of fruit. Cover page 35 and then read aloud page 34. *What does this page show? The author says she likes yellow, but that she likes green more. What do you think the next page will show? What clues help you to know that?*   Uncover and read page 35 to confirm children's predictions.

 ### Comprehension Focus: Sequence of Events

Student Modeling Sometimes authors give you clues about what will be shown next. Ask: *What does the author say on page 34 that helps you know what fruit will be shown next page?*

page 36

Strategy: Predict/Infer

■ *The author likes orange, but she says she likes red more. What do you think the next page will show? Why do you say that?*

page 37

Compare and Contrast

■ *What other fruits can you name that are red? Which of these fruits do you like best? Why?*

These bananas are yellow.
I like yellow, but I like green more.

These pears are green.
I like green, but I like orange more.

pages 34–35

These oranges are orange.
I like orange, but I like red more.

These cherries are red.
Red is my favorite color because...

pages 36–37

cherries are my favorite fruit!
What color is your favorite fruit?

page 38

Revisiting the Text

pages 37–38

Concepts of Print

 Capitalize First Word in Sentence; End Punctuation

■ Frame and read: *Cherries are red. Why does* Cherries *begin with a capital letter?*

■ Recall that all sentences end with a mark. *The sentence (Cherries are red.) is a telling sentence so it ends with a period.*

■ Frame the second sentence on page 38 and read it aloud. *This sentence asks a question. What mark do we use at the end of a sentence that asks a question?*

▶ Responding

Summarizing Have children summarize the selection, using the pictures as prompts.

 Extra Support

Some children may not be familiar with all the different fruits shown in the article. Prior to reading, children may benefit from describing and tasting actual fruits or looking at fruits in other books.

 Challenge

Prepare cards for the words and end marks for several sentences from the selection. One child can build a sentence and a partner can find it in the book.

DAY 4

Sharing the Big Book (T41)

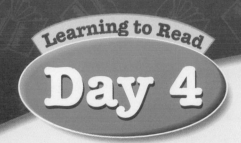
OBJECTIVES

Children

- identify words that begin with /s/

- identify pictures whose names start with the letter *s*

MATERIALS

- **Alphafriend Card** *Sammy Seal*

- **Alphafolder** *Sammy Seal*

- *From Apples to Zebras: A Book of ABC's,* page 20

- **Letter Card** *s*

- **Picture Cards** *bug, map, red, sad, salt, sandals, red, tent*

- **Phonics Center:** Theme 2, Week 1, Day 4

Home Connection

Ask children to look at home for items or for names that begin with the letter s. Children can draw pictures to show what they have found.

Phonics

✓ Review Initial Consonant s

▶ Develop Phonemic Awareness

Beginning Sound Display the scene in Sammy Seal's Alphafolder. *One thing I see in the picture is a surfboard. Say* surfboard *with me. Does* surfboard *begin with the same sound as Sammy Seal, /s/?*

Call on volunteers to point to and name other items in the picture that begin with /s/.

▶ Connect Sounds to Letters

Review Consonant s Using self-stick notes, cover the words on page 20 of *From Apples to Zebras: A Book of ABC's*. Then display the page. Ask children what letter they expect to see at the beginning of each word and why. Uncover the words so that children can check their predictions.

Provide each child with a self-stick note. Ask children to write the letter *s* on their notes. Then have children place their notes on objects in the classroom that begin with /s/. Allow children to mark the same item.

Confirm children's decisions by listing the words for the items they marked on the board. Call on volunteers to underline the *s* in each word you write.

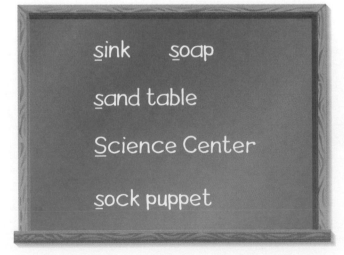

s̲ink   s̲oap

s̲and table

S̲cience Center

s̲ock puppet

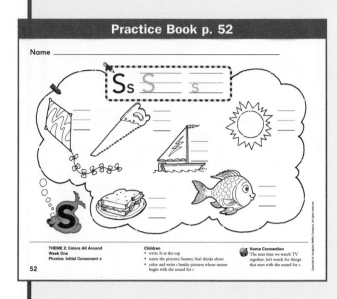

▶ Apply

In a pocket chart, display the card for *Sammy Seal* and the Letter Card *s.*

Hold up Picture Cards one at a time. Children signal "thumbs up" for pictures that start with Sammy Seal's sound, /s/. Repeat the word emphasizing initial /s/ as you place the picture under the letter *s.* Children signal "thumbs down" for pictures that do not begin with /s/.

Pictures: *sandals, map, tent, six, red, sad, bug, salt.*

Tell children they will sort more pictures in the Phonics Center today.

Practice Book page 52 Children will complete this page at small group time.

Phonics Library In groups today, children will also identify words that begin with initial *s* as they reread the **Phonics Library** story "My Red Boat." See suggestions, page T35.

At Group Time

Phonics Center

Use the Phonics Center materials for **Theme 2, Week 1, Day 4**.

Practice Book p. 52

Name _____

DAY 4

Diagnostic Check

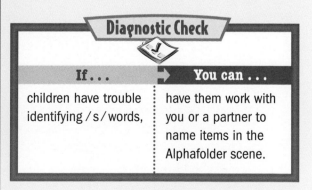

If . . .	You can . . .
children have trouble identifying /s/ words,	have them work with you or a partner to name items in the Alphafolder scene.

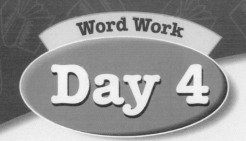

Word Work

Day 4

OBJECTIVES

Children
- explore color words

MATERIALS

Big Book: *What's My Favorite Color?*

Exploring Words

▶ Color Words

Display the color chart children made with you during yesterday's Word Work activity. Read the chart with them, emphasizing the color words.

■ Recall that in *What's My Favorite Color?* the author named different fruits that are usually known for being certain colors.

■ As children brainstorm other foods that are the same colors, create a chart.

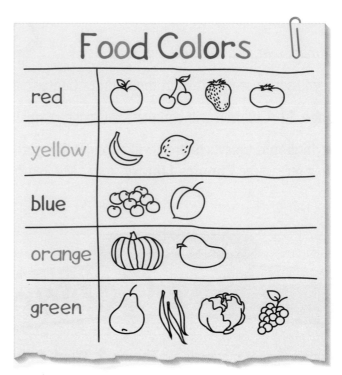

Interactive Writing

▶ Writing a Description

Viewing and Speaking Share pages 2–5 of *I Went Walking*. Have children use color words to describe what they see.

Display the chart from yesterday's shared writing. Review what children saw on their walk. Tell children that they will write a class story using the pattern in *I Went Walking*.

■ Write the following sentences on chart paper: *I went walking. What did you see? I saw a _____.* Model how to complete the sentence, using an item from the walk. Then read the sentences, adding the item you chose.

■ Continue writing the class story, having the children contribute their ideas. Share the pen by having children add punctuation and write *I* or the initial letter *s*.

OBJECTIVES

Children
- use color words in an oral context
- innovate text to create a class story

MATERIALS

- **Big Book:** *I Went Walking*

Portfolio Opportunity
Save children's writing as examples of their ability to innovate text.

At Group Time

Writing Center

Materials • Blackline Master 35

Place copies of **Blackline Master 35,** the Our Class Walk chart, and the *I Went Walking* story in the Writing Center. Children can draw a picture or write the words to complete **Blackline Master 35.** Some children may wish to make their own books.

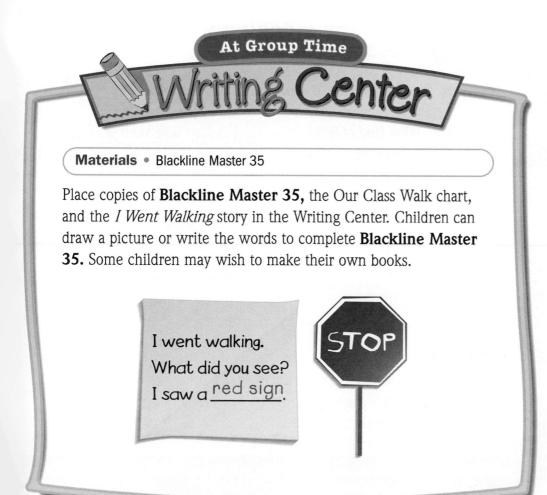

I went walking.
What did you see?
I saw a red sign.

DAY 4

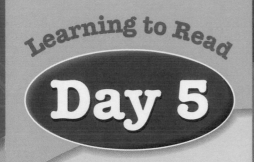

Day 5

Day at a Glance

Learning to Read

Revisiting the Literature:

I Need a Lunch Box, I Went Walking, What's My Favorite Color?, "My Red Boat"

✓ **Phonics: Initial Consonant s,** *page T50*

Word Work

Exploring Words, *page T52*

Writing & Language

Independent Writing, *page T53*

 Half-Day Kindergarten

✓ Indicates lessons for tested skills. Choose additional activities as time allows.

Opening

Calendar

Sunday	Monday	Tuesday	Wednesday	Thursday	Friday	Saturday
			1	2	3	4
5	6	7	8	9	10	11
12	13	14	15	16	17	18
19	20	21	22	23	24	25
26	27	28	29	30	31	

Use the color of the day to mark the calendar and launch children into sharing the colored items they've worn or brought in. Make children aware of shades of color. *Tula's rubber duck is a bright yellow, like the sun. Mark's shirt is a golden yellow, like honey.*

Daily Message

Modeled Writing As you write the daily message, call on children to help you. *What kind of letter should I use to begin my sentence? Is this a telling or asking sentence? Should I put a period or a question mark at the end?*

Today we will go to the library.

How many books do you think you will borrow?

Share this riddle with children. *I am a letter, but I am also a word. I am always spelled with a capital. Who am I?* When children guess *I*, have a volunteer point to *I* on the Word Wall.

Daily Phonemic Awareness
Beginning Sounds

- Play a guessing game to call attention to the beginning sounds in names. Choose a name that begins with /s/. Say: *I am thinking of someone's name in this room. The name starts with /s/. Who has a name that starts with /s/?*

- Allow children to guess all the possibilities before revealing the name you had in mind.

- Repeat several times until children have guessed all of the /s/ names.

Syllables in Spoken Words

- *Let's play a clapping game. Listen:* vi-o-let. *Say and clap the color with me. How many claps did you hear? Yes, three.*

- Repeat with other color words.

Getting Ready to Learn

To help plan their day, tell children that they will

- reread and talk about all the books they've read this week.

- take home a story they can read.

- write about their favorite foods in their journals.

My Red Boat
by Susan Gorman-Howe
illustrated by Lauren Scheuer

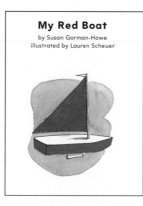

DAY 5

Revisiting the Literature

▶ Literature Discussion

Today children will compare the different books you shared this week: *I Need a Lunch Box, I Went Walking, What's My Favorite Color?* and "My Red Boat." First, use these suggestions to help children recall the selections:

- Have volunteers tell why the boy in *I Need a Lunch Box* wanted a lunch box. Ask what was unusual about the boy's dream.

- Ask children to recall the animals the boy in *I Went Walking* saw on his walk.

- Have children recall *What's My Favorite Color?* Select children to find their favorite fruits and colors in the selection.

- Together read "My Red Boat." Ask volunteers to name the / s / objects in the story.

- Ask children to vote for their favorite book of the week, and then read the winner aloud.

✓ Comprehension: Sequence of Events

Comparing Books Remind children that knowing the order in which things happen can help them to better understand and enjoy a story. Browse through each selection, inviting comments about how children used the sequence of events to help them make predictions. After looking at each story, help children develop a one- or two-sentence summary.

Technology

www.eduplace.com
Log on to **Education Place** for more activities relating to Colors All Around.

www.bookadventure.org
This Internet reading-incentive program provides thousands of titles for children to read.

Building Fluency

▶ Rereading Familiar Texts

Phonics Library: "My Red Boat" Remind children that they've learned the sound for *s*, /s/. As children reread the **Phonics Library** story "My Red Boat," have them look for pictures that begin with /s/.

Review Feature several familiar **Phonics Library** titles in the Book Corner. Have children demonstrate their growing skills by choosing one to describe the pictures, alternating pages with a partner.

Oral Reading Frequent rereadings of familiar texts help children develop their vocabulary. Model how to describe the illustration expressively. Then have children try it.

My Red Boat
by Susan Gorman-Howe
illustrated by Lauren Scheuer

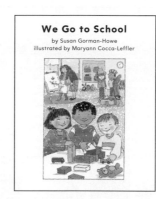

We Go to School
by Susan Gorman-Howe
illustrated by Maryann Cocca-Leffler

We Can Make It
by Susan Gorman-Howe
illustrated by Anthony Lewis

Blackline Master 36 Children complete the page and take it home to share their reading progress.

My Reading Log

My new word

Leveled Books

The materials listed below provide reading practice for children at different levels.

Little Big Books

I Went Walking

WRITTEN BY
Sue Williams

ILLUSTRATED BY
Julie Vivas

Little Readers for Guided Reading

Houghton Mifflin Classroom Bookshelf

DAY 5

Home Connection

Remind children to share the take-home version of "My Red Boat" with their families.

Phonics Review

☑ Initial Consonant s

OBJECTIVES

◎

Children

- review initial consonant *s*
- review letter names
- make sentences with high-frequency word *I*

MATERIALS

- **Word Card** *I*
- **Picture Cards** for *s* and assorted others; *cut, dig, hop, hug, run*
- **Punctuation Card:** period

▶ Review

Tell children that they will take turns naming pictures that begin with /s/ and writing the letter that stands for /s/.

- ■ Place two Picture Cards, one for *s* and one distractor, along the chalkboard ledge. Choose a volunteer to name each picture, and write *s* above the /s/ picture. Then have the rest of the class verify that *s* has been written above the correct picture. Write the picture name on the board. Choose another volunteer to underline the initial consonant *s*.

- ■ Continue until everyone has a chance to write or underline *s*.

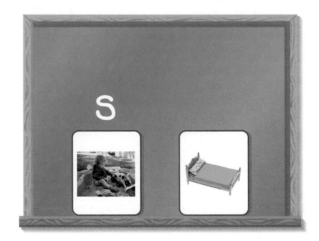

▶ Review Letter Names

- ■ Recite the alphabet together with the children.
- ■ Hold up Letter Cards at random and have children name them.

High-Frequency Word Review

▶ Review

Give each small group of children the Word Cards, Picture Cards, and Punctuation Card needed to make a sentence. Each child holds one card. Children stand and arrange themselves to make a sentence for others to read.

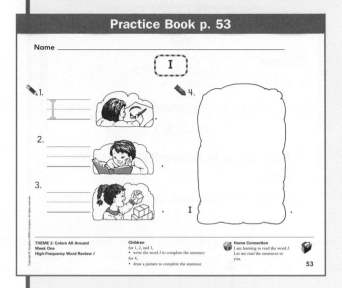

Portfolio Opportunity

Add the Practice Book page to children's portfolios as a sample of what they have learned.

▶ Apply

Practice Book page 53 Children can complete this page independently and read it to you during small group time.

Phonics Library Have children take turns telling a story to the class. Each child might summarize one page of "My Red Boat" or a favorite **Phonics Library** selection from the previous theme. Remind readers to share the pictures!

Questions for discussion:

■ *What objects can you find that start with the same sound as Sammy Seal's name? What is the letter? What is the sound?*

■ *Why is this your favorite Phonics Library story?*

Diagnostic Check

If...	➡ You can...
children need help remembering the sound for consonant *s*,	have them listen to Sammy Seal's song and listen for *s* words.

DAY 5

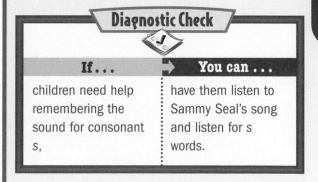

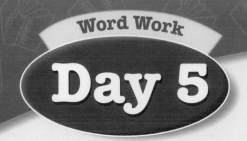

Exploring Words

▶ Color Words

Display page 29 of *From Apples to Zebras: A Book of ABC's.* Call on volunteers to point to and name the colors on the page.

■ Then ask children what colors they see when they look at the sky. Ask: *What color is the daytime sky? the nighttime sky? What color is the sun? the moon? the stars? Have you ever looked at the sky and seen lots of different colors? What colors did you see?*

■ If children do not mention a rainbow in the discussion, encourage children who have seen rainbows to tell about them. Then display a photograph or a picture of a rainbow and have children name the colors in the rainbow.

Writing Opportunity Have children draw or paint their own rainbows. They can label the colors in their rainbows by referring to the class color chart or page 29 of *From Apples to Zebras: A Book of ABC's.*

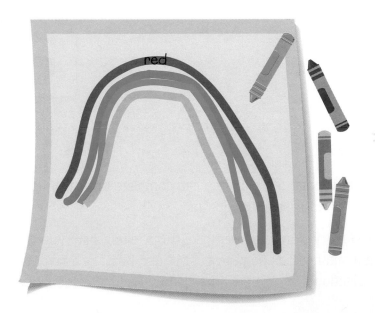

Independent Writing

Journals Review the charts from this week's shared and interactive writing activities. Point out the color words.

- Distribute the journals, and tell children that today's journal entry will be about their favorite color.

- Remind them that they can use the Word Wall, the story charts, and the color word lists to help them write words.

- Invite children to share their journals in small groups.

I like yellow.

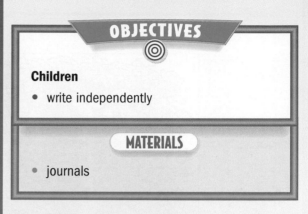

OBJECTIVES

Children
- write independently

MATERIALS
- journals

 Portfolio Opportunity

Mark journal entries you would like to share with parents. Allow children to indicate their best efforts or favorite works for sharing as well.

Literature for Week 2
Different texts for different purposes

Teacher Read Aloud

Purposes

- oral language
- listening strategy
- comprehension skill

Big Books:

Higglety Pigglety: A Book of Rhymes

Purposes

- oral language development
- phonemic awareness

From Apples to Zebras: A Book of ABC's

Purposes

- alphabet recognition
- letters and sounds

In the Big Blue Sea

by Chyng Feng Sun
Photography by Norbert Wu

Includes: Science Link

Big Book: Main Selection

Purposes

- concepts of print
- reading strategy
- story language
- comprehension skills

Also available in Little Big Book and audiotape

Leveled Books

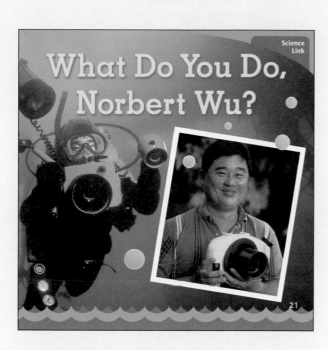

Also in the Big Book:
– Science Link

Purposes

- reading strategies
- comprehension skills
- concepts of print

Phonics Library

Also available in Take-Home version

Purpose

- applying phonics skills and high-frequency words

On My Way Paperback

Beautiful Butterflies
by **Demaris Tyler**
page T153

Little Readers for Guided Reading
Collection K

Houghton Mifflin Classroom Bookshelf
Level K

Technology

www.eduplace.com

Log on to *Education Place* for more activities relating to *Colors All Around.*

www.bookadventure.org

This free Internet reading incentive program provides thousands of titles for students to read.

Suggested Daily Routines

Instructional Goals

Learning to Read

☑ *Phonemic Awareness:* Beginning Sounds, Syllables in Spoken Words

Strategy Focus: Summarize

☑ *Comprehension Skill:* Inferences: Making Predictions

☑ *Phonics Skills*

Phonemic Awareness: Beginning Sound /m/

Initial Consonant *M, m*

Compare and Review: Initial Consonant: *s*

☑ *High-Frequency Word:* see

☑ *Concepts of Print:* Capitalize First Word in Sentences; End Punctuation

Word Work

High-Frequency Word Practice: Color Words

Writing & Language

Vocabulary Skill: Using Exact Naming Words

Writing Skill: Writing a Description

☑ = tested skills

Leveled Books

Have children read in appropriate levels daily.

Phonics Library
On My Way Practice Readers
Little Big Books
Houghton Mifflin Classroom Bookshelf

Day 1

Opening Routines, *T60–T61*

Word Wall

• **Phonemic Awareness:** Beginning Sounds, Syllables in Spoken Words

Teacher Read Aloud
Caps of Many Colors, T62–T65
• **Strategy:** Summarize
• **Comprehension:** Inferences: Making Predictions

Phonics
Instruction
• Phonemic Awareness, Beginning Sound /m/, *T66–T67; Practice Book, 57–58*

High-Frequency Word Practice
• Word: *I, T68*

Oral Language
• Using Exact Naming Words, *T69*
• Listening and Speaking, *T69*

Managing Small Groups
Teacher-Led Group
• Reread familiar **Phonics Library** selections

Independent Groups
• Finish *Practice Book, 55–58*
• *Phonics Center:* Theme 2, Week 2, Day 1
• Book, Dramatic Play, Writing, other Centers

Day 2

Opening Routines, *T70–T71*

Word Wall

• **Phonemic Awareness:** Beginning Sounds, Syllables in Spoken Words

Sharing the Big Book
In the Big Blue Sea, T72–T73
• **Strategy:** Summarize
• **Comprehension:** Inferences: Making Predictions

Phonics
Instruction, Practice
• Initial Consonant *m, T74–T75*
• *Practice Book, 59*

High-Frequency Word
• New Word: *see, T76–T77*
• *Practice Book, 60*

High-Frequency Word Practice
• Building Sentences, *T78*

Vocabulary Expansion
• Using Exact Naming Words, *T79*
• Viewing and Speaking, *T79*

Managing Small Groups
Teacher-Led Group
• Begin *Practice Book, 59–60* and handwriting Blackline Masters 169 or 195.
Independent Groups
• Finish *Practice Book, 59–60* and handwriting Blackline Masters 169 or 195.
• *Phonics Center:* Theme 2, Week 2, Day 2
• Science, Book, other Centers

Technology

Lesson Planner CD-ROM: Customize your planning for *Colors All Around* with the Lesson Planner.

Day 3

Opening Routines, *T80–T81*

Word Wall

• **Phonemic Awareness:** Beginning Sounds, Syllables in Spoken Words

Sharing the Big Book
In the Big Blue Sea, T82–T85
• **Strategy:** Summarize
• **Comprehension:** Inferences: Making Predictions, *T83*; *Practice Book, 61*
• **Concepts of Print:** Capitalize First Word in Sentence; End Punctuation, *T84*

Phonics
Practice, Application
• Initial Consonant *m, T88–T89*

Instruction
• Beginning Letter *m, T88–T89*
• **Phonics Library:** "Look at Me," *T89*

Exploring Words
• Color Words, *T90*

✎ **Shared Writing**
• Writing a Description, *T91*
• Viewing and Speaking, *T91*

Managing Small Groups
Teacher-Led Group
• Read **Phonics Library** selection "Look at Me"
• Begin *Practice Book, 61*

Independent Groups
• Finish *Practice Book, 61*
• Art, other Centers

Day 4

Opening Routines, *T92–T93*

Word Wall

• **Phonemic Awareness:** Beginning Sounds, Syllables in Spoken Words

Sharing the Big Book
Science Link: "What Do You Do, Norbert Wu?," *T94–T95*
• **Strategy:** Summarize
• **Comprehension:** Inferences: Making Predictions
• **Concepts of Print:** Capitalize First Word in Sentence; End Punctuation

Phonics
Practice
• Review Initial Consonant *m, T96–T97*; *Practice Book, 62*

Exploring Words
• Color Words, *T98*

✎ **Interactive Writing**
• Writing a Description, *T99*

Managing Small Groups
Teacher-Led Group
• Reread **Phonics Library** selection "Look at Me"
• Begin *Practice Book, 62*

Independent Groups
• Finish *Practice Book, 62*
• *Phonics Center:* Theme 2, Week 2, Day 4
• Other Centers

Day 5

Opening Routines, *T100–T101*

Word Wall

• **Phonemic Awareness:** Beginning Sounds, Syllables in Spoken Words

Revisiting the Literature
Comprehension: Inferences: Making Predictions, *T102*

Building Fluency
• **Phonics Library:** "Look at Me," *T103*

Phonics
Review
• Initial Consonants: *m, s, T104*

High-Frequency Word Review
• Words: *I, see, T105*; *Practice Book, 63*

Exploring Words
• Color Words, *T106*

✎ **Independent Writing**
• Journals: Write About Something You Learned, *T107*

Managing Small Groups
Teacher-Led Group
• Reread familiar **Phonics Library** selections
• Begin *Practice Book, 63*, Blackline Master 36.

Independent Groups
• Reread **Phonics Library** selections
• Finish *Practice Book, 63*, Blackline Master 36.
• Centers

Setting up the Centers

Management Tip Make extra copies of **Blackline Masters 37 and 38.** The fish shapes on these blackline masters are used in two activities this week, so it will be helpful to have extra copies on hand.

Phonics Center

Materials • Phonics Center materials for Theme 2, Week 2

Pairs work together to sort Picture Cards by initial sound. See pages T67, T75, and T97 for this week's Phonics Center activities.

black bear

Writing Center

Materials • Kinds of Animals chart from Day 1 • drawing paper • markers

Children draw pictures of animals listed on the Kinds of Animals chart. Children may also label their pictures with a color word. See page T69 for this week's Writing Center activity.

Book Center

Materials • *In the Big Blue Sea*

Children work in pairs to compare and contrast the fish pictured in the glossary. Then they look for the different fish in the book and record where the fish appear. See page T79 for this week's Book Center activity.

Dramatic Play Center

Children will enjoy working in small groups to dramatize the story *Caps of Many Colors.* See page T63 for this week's Dramatic Play Center activity.

Science Center

Materials • nonfiction picture books about fish • mural paper • water colors • Blackline Masters 37–38

Children create a class mural about fish. They can paint the sea background and add a variety of colored fish using **Blackline Masters 37–38.** See page T73 for this week's Science Center activity.

Art Center

Materials • Blackline Masters 37–38 • paints and brushes • crayons • markers • coat hangers • string

Children create fish mobiles using **Blackline Masters 37–38.** Children look at the glossary in *In the Big Blue Sea* and paint the fish in similar patterns. Then they hang their fish from coat hangers to complete their mobiles. See T87 for this week's Art Center activity.

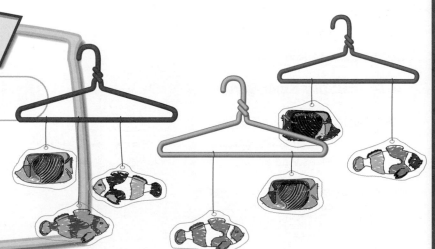

Day 1

Day at a Glance

Learning to Read

Teacher Read Aloud:

Caps of Many Colors

 Learning About /m/, page T66

Word Work

High-Frequency Word Practice, page T68

Writing & Language

Oral Language, page T69

Half-Day Kindergarten

✓ Indicates lessons for tested skills. Choose additional activities as time allows.

Opening

Calendar

Sunday	Monday	Tuesday	Wednesday	Thursday	Friday	Saturday
			1	2	3	4
5	6	7	8	9	10	11
12	13	14	15	16	17	18
19	20	21	22	23	24	25
26	27	28	29	30	31	

Discuss today's date. Count the number of Mondays that are in the month. Ask children what they did over the weekend. Have them include any colors they may have seen while they were outside on Saturday and Sunday.

Daily Message

Modeled Writing As an introduction to today's story, incorporate the colors of children's hats or baseball caps into the daily message.

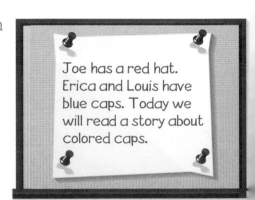

Joe has a red hat. Erica and Louis have blue caps. Today we will read a story about colored caps.

Ask children to find and read the word they added to the Word Wall last week. Then chant the spelling of the word with children: *capital* I *spells* I, *capital* I *spells* I.

Daily Phonemic Awareness

Beginning Sounds

* *Listen:* book, bed. *Say the words with me:* book, bed. *Do* book *and* bed *begin with the same sound? Yes,* book *and* bed *both begin with* /b/.

* Tell children that they will now Same Sound Sort. *If the words begin with the same sound, raise your hand. If the words do not begin with the same sound, cover your ears.*

 Syllables in Spoken Words

* *Last week, you clapped the sounds in your first names. Today, you will clap the sounds in your last names.*

* Choose a child with a two-syllable last name and say the name aloud: *Da-vis*. Say the name again, clapping the syllables. *How many claps did you hear? Yes, two! Now say and clap the name with me:* Da-vis.

* Continue with other children's last names.

cup/cat	dish/bowl
red/room	sun/rabbit
seal/safe	milk/juice
moon/mat	box/bath

Getting Ready to Learn

To help plan their day, tell children that they will

* listen to a story called *Caps of Many Colors*.

* meet a new Alphafriend, Mimi Mouse.

* draw animal pictures in Writing Center.

black bear

Day 1

Read Aloud

Purposes • oral language • listening strategy • comprehension skill

Selection Summary

A cap peddler awakens from a nap to find that monkeys in the tree above him have stolen his caps. Furious, the peddler yells, shakes his fists, and stamps his feet, but the monkeys just mimic him. In frustration, he throws his own cap to the ground and, when the monkeys do the same, retrieves all his caps.

Key Concept

Playing tricks

 MEETING INDIVIDUAL NEEDS

English Language Learners

This selection presents challenging vocabulary. Before you read, review or introduce a few words: *goods, stack, shade (of color), topple off, balanced, monkeys,* and *fist.*

Teacher Read Aloud
Oral Language/Comprehension

▶ **Building Background**

Have children tell about monkeys they've seen. Point out that monkeys can do many things humans can because, unlike other animals, they can hold things in their hands. Display *Caps of Many Colors* and read the title aloud. Have children comment on the story art, pointing out the caps and the price tags. Lead children to see that this man sells caps.

Strategy: Summarize

Teacher Modeling Model the Summarize strategy for children.

Think Aloud

When I summarize a story, I tell about the important parts that I have read. As I read, I'll remember the order of what happens. You help me do this, too.

✓ Comprehension Focus: Inferences: Making Predictions

Teacher Modeling Remind children that good readers think about, or predict, what will happen next in a story. They then check their predictions as they read.

Think Aloud

When I look at this picture, I see the man with the caps under a tree. I also see something in the tree over the man's head. Can you guess what is in the tree? Let's read to see if your prediction is correct.

▶ Listening to the Story

Read the story aloud, emphasizing the actions of the man and the reactions of the monkeys. Pause at the discussion points and allow children to predict what they think will happen next. Note that the Read Aloud art is also available on the back of the Theme poster.

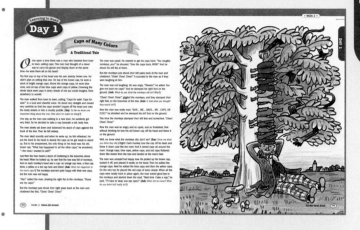

▶ Responding

Summarizing the Story Help children summarize parts of the story.

■ *What happened as the man slept under the tree?*

■ *What did the man do when he saw that the monkeys had taken his caps? What did the monkeys do?*

■ *How did the man get his caps back? Do you think the man planned to do this? Why or why not?*

■ *What was your favorite part of the story?*

Practice Book pages 55–56 Children will complete the pages during small group time.

Practice Book p. 56

Name _____

Practice Book p. 55

Name _____

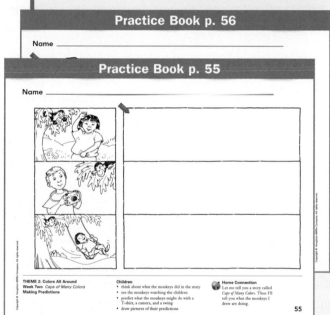

THEME 2: Colors All Around
Week Two *Caps of Many Colors*
Making Predictions

Children
• think about what the monkeys did in the story
• see the monkeys watching the children
• predict what the monkeys might do with a T-shirt, a camera, and a swing
• draw pictures of their predictions

Home Connection
Let me tell you a story called *Caps of Many Colors*. Then I'll tell you what the monkeys I drew are doing.

55

At Group Time

Materials • construction paper

Children can act out *Caps of Many Colors* in the Dramatic Play Center. They can make construction paper caps and use them during their dramatization.

Extra Support

Children who need help summarizing the story may benefit from seeing the illustrations in a picture book retelling of the story, such as *Caps for Sale* by Esphyr Slobodkina.

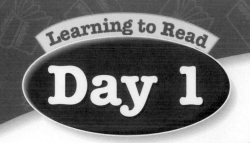

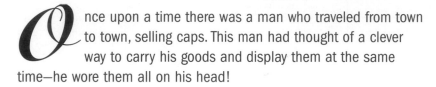

Caps of Many Colors

A Traditional Tale

Once upon a time there was a man who traveled from town to town, selling caps. This man had thought of a clever way to carry his goods and display them at the same time—he wore them all on his head!

The first cap on top of his head was his own shabby brown one. He didn't plan on selling that one. On top of the brown cap, he wore a stack of bright orange caps. Above the orange caps, he wore blue ones, and on top of the blue caps were caps of yellow. Crowning the whole stack were caps in every shade of red you could imagine, from strawberry to scarlet.

The man walked from town to town, calling, "Caps for sale! Caps for sale!" in a loud and cheerful voice. He stood very straight and moved very carefully so that the caps wouldn't topple off his head and onto the dusty streets or into a muddy puddle. **(Say:** *So far we know one important thing about the man. How does he make his living?***)**

One day, as the man was walking to a new town, he suddenly got very tired. So he decided to take a nap beneath a tall, leafy tree.

The man slowly sat down and balanced his stack of caps against the trunk of the tree. Then he fell asleep.

The man slept soundly and when he woke up, he felt refreshed. He put his hand to his head to steady the caps as he got ready to stand up. But to his amazement, the only thing on his head was his old, brown cap. "What has happened to all the other caps," he wondered, "—the ones I wanted to sell?"

Just then the man heard a storm of chattering in the branches above his head. When he looked up, he saw that the tree was full of *monkeys.* And on each monkey's head was a cap: an orange cap here, a blue cap there, a yellow or a red cap here and there! **(Ask:** *What has happened to the man's caps?***)** The monkeys seemed quite happy with their new caps, but the man was not happy.

"Hey!" called the man, shaking his right fist at the monkeys, "Those are my caps!"

But the monkeys just shook *their* right paws back at the man and chattered like this, "Chee! Chee! Chee!"

The man was upset. He needed to get his caps back. "You naughty monkeys, you!" he shouted. "Give the caps back, NOW!" And he shook his left fist at them.

But the monkeys just shook *their* left paws back at the man and chattered, "Chee! Chee! Chee!" It sounded to the man as if they were laughing at him.

The man was not laughing. He was angry. "Thieves!" he yelled. You give me back my caps!" And he stamped his *right* foot on the ground. **(Ask:** *What do you think the monkeys will do? Why?***)**

"Chee! Chee! Chee!" giggled the monkeys, and they stamped *their* right feet on the branches of the tree. **(Ask:** *Is that what you thought they would do?***)**

Now the man was really mad. "GIVE... ME... BACK... MY... CAPS, OR ELSE!" he shrieked and he stamped his *left* foot on the ground.

This time the monkeys stamped *their* left feet and screeched, "Chee! Chee! Chee!"

Now the man was so angry, and so upset, and so frustrated, that without thinking he tore his old brown cap off his head and threw it on the ground.

Well, *we* know what the monkeys did, don't we? **(Say:** *Show me what you think they did.***)** Right! Each monkey tore the cap off its head and threw it down—just like the man! And it rained caps all around the man! Orange caps, blue caps, yellow caps, and red caps fluttered down like leaves from the tree and landed at the man's feet.

The man was amazed but happy now. He picked up his brown cap, dusted it off, and placed it neatly on his head. Then he added the orange caps. Next he added the blue caps and then the yellow caps. On the very top he placed the red caps of every shade. When all the caps were neatly back in place again, the man waved good-bye to the monkeys and started down the road. "Next time I take a nap," he said, "I'll have to keep one eye open!" **(Ask:** *What did he mean? What do you think he'll really do?***)**

OBJECTIVES

Children

- identify pictures whose names begin with /m/

MATERIALS

- **Alphafriend Cards** *Mimi Mouse, Sammy Seal*
- **Alphafriend Audiotape** Theme 2
- **Alphafolder** *Mimi Mouse*
- **Picture Cards** *man, map, mule, seal, six, sun*
- **Phonics Center:** Theme 2, Week 2, Day 1

Home Connection

A take-home version of Mimi Mouse's Song is on an **Alphafriends Blackline Master**. Children can share the song with their families.

English Language Learners

Ask children to name things around the classroom that begin with the /m/ sound. Then ask, *Does anyone's name begin with /m/?*

Phonemic Awareness

✓ Beginning Sound

▶ Introducing the Alphafriend: Mimi Mouse

Tell children that today they will meet a new Alphafriend. Recall with children that Alphafriends are friends that help them to remember the sounds the letters of the alphabet make. Have children listen as you share a riddle to help them guess who their new Alphafriend is.

1 **Alphafriend Riddle** Read these clues:

- *Our Alphafriend's sound is /m/. Say it with me: /m/.*
- *This tiny animal has big ears and a small tail.*
- *She loves to nibble cheese and other snacks.*
- *She "squeaks" when she sees a cat and runs to hide.*

When most hands are up, call on children until they guess *mouse*.

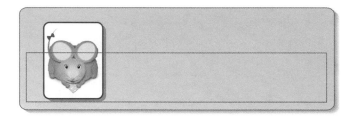

2 **Pocket Chart** Display Mimi Mouse in a pocket chart. Say her name, stretching the /m/ sound slightly, and have children echo.

3 📼 **Alphafriend Audiotape** Play Mimi Mouse's song. *Listen for /m/ words in Mimi's song.*

4 **Alphafolder** Have children find the /m/ pictures in the scene.

5 **Summarize**

- *What is our Alphafriend's name? What is her sound?*
- *What words in our Alphafriend's song start with /m/?*
- *Each time you look at Mimi Mouse this week, remember the /m/ sound.*

Mimi Mouse's Song
(Tune: "This Old Man")

Mimi Mouse, Mimi Mouse,
Minds her manners in the house
When she sips her milk,
   she never makes a mess.
Mud pies never stain
   her dress.

▶ Listening for / m /

Compare and Review: / s / Display Alphafriend *Sammy Seal* opposite *Mimi Mouse*. Review each character's sound.

Tell children you'll name some pictures and they should signal "thumbs up" for each one that begins like Mimi's name. Volunteers put the card below Mimi's picture. For "thumbs down" words, volunteers state the beginning sound, / s /, and place the cards below Sammy's picture.

Pictures: *man, map, mule, seal, six, sun*

Tell children they will sort more pictures in the Phonics Center today.

▶ Apply

Practice Book pages 57–58 Children will complete the pages at small group time.

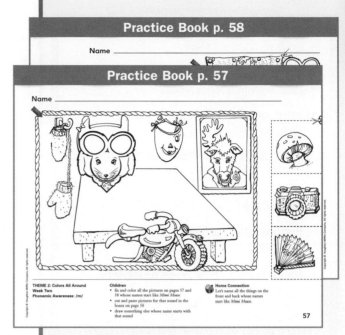

At Group Time

Phonics Center

Use the Phonics Center materials for **Theme 2, Week 2, Day 1**.

Day 1

OBJECTIVES

Children

- read high-frequency words
- create and write sentences with high-frequency words

MATERIALS

- **Word Card** *I*
- **Picture Cards** *cut, dig, hop, hug, kiss, mix, run, zip*
- *Higglety Pigglety: A Book of Rhymes,* page 10
- **Punctuation Card:** period

High-Frequency Word Practice

▶ Matching Words

- Display the Word Card for the high-frequency word *I* in a pocket chart. Have children read the word and match it on the Word Wall.

- Remind children that the word *I* is often found in books. *I'll read a poem. You listen to hear if this word is used in it.*

- Read the poem "I Love Colors" on page 10 of *Higglety Pigglety. Did you hear the word* I *in the poem? Let's see if you can match the Word Card* I *to the word* I *in the poem.*

I LOVE COLORS

I love colors, yes I do!
Red and orange and green and blue!
I love colors, dark or bright,
Yellow, purple, black, and white!
by Meish Goldish

10

Higglety Pigglety: A Book of Rhymes, page 10

Writing Opportunity Place the Word Card *I* in a pocket chart. Then display the Picture Cards *cut, dig, hop, hug, kiss, mix, run,* and *zip.* Help children build sentences with the Word and Picture Cards. Children may then write and illustrate one of the sentences or use the cards to create their own sentences with rebus pictures.

Oral Language

▶ Using Exact Naming Words

Listening and Speaking Tell children that some words are naming words, or nouns. *The word* animal *is a naming word.*

■ Tell children that some naming words are more exact than others. *Think about the word* animal. *When you think about that word, what animals come to mind?*

■ Write children's responses on a chart titled *Kinds of Animals.*

Portfolio Opportunity
Save children's work as examples of their drawing and writing abilities.

At Group Time
Writing Center

Materials • drawing paper • crayons and markers

Put the chart in the Writing Center. Children can draw and label their own animal pictures. If children want to include color words in their writing, they can refer to the posted color chart.

black bear

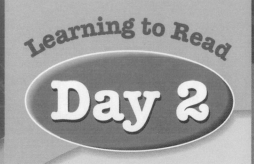

Day at a Glance

Learning to Read

Big Book:

In the Big Blue Sea

✓ **Phonics: Initial Consonant *m*,** page T74

✓ **High-Frequency Word: *see*,** page T76

Word Work

High-Frequency Word Practice, *page T76*

Writing & Language

Vocabulary Expansion, *page T79*

 Half-Day Kindergarten

✓ Indicates lessons for tested skills. Choose additional activities as time allows.

Opening

Calendar

Sunday	Monday	Tuesday	Wednesday	Thursday	Friday	Saturday
			1	2	3	4
5	6	7	8	9	10	11
12	13	14	15	16	17	18
19	20	21	22	23	24	25
26	27	28	29	30	31	

Write today's date on the board. Ask children to find it on the calendar, and then name yesterday's date and tomorrow's date. Ask several volunteers to tell what plans they have for after school.

Daily Message

Modeled Writing Select two colors, for example, green and blue. Count how many children have on green and how many have on blue. Use this information in the daily message. *The first word I want to write is six. Since six is the first word in my sentence, I will begin it with a capital letter. What letter stands for the sound at the beginning of six?*

> Six children are wearing green. Seven children are wearing blue today.

Have children find and read the word they added to the Word Wall last week. Chant the spelling of the word with children: *capitol I spells I.*

Routines

 ## Daily Phonemic Awareness
Beginning Sounds

- *Tell me which word begins with Mimi Mouse's sound, /m/. Listen:* man, jam.

- *Say the words:* man, jam. *Which word begins with /m/? Yes,* man.

- Continue with the words shown.

 ## Syllables in Spoken Words

- Read aloud "I Went Upstairs" on page 12 of *Higglety Pigglety.*

- Tell children that today they'll clap the word parts they hear in words from the poem.

- *Listen:* mis-take. Say *mistake* again, clapping the syllables. *How may claps did you hear? Yes, two! Now say and clap the word with me:* mis-take.

- Continue with other words from the poem.

broom/moon
sing/more
mat/juice
line/mouth
jump/milk
mine/lunch
car/mop
Monday/sleep
rug/march

Getting Ready to Learn

To help plan their day, tell children that they will

- listen to a Big Book: *In the Big Blue Sea.*

- learn the new letters, *M* and *m,* and see words that begin with *m.*

- explore fish in the Science Center.

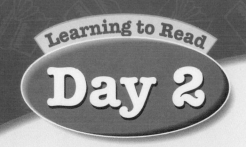

Big Book

In the Big Blue Sea

by Chyng Feng Sun
Photography by Norbert Wu

Purposes • concepts of print • story language
• reading strategy • comprehension skill

Selection Summary
In this photo essay, children are invited to accompany Norbert Wu as he photographs colorful fish in the ocean.

Key Concepts
Shapes, sizes, and colors of fish

MEETING INDIVIDUAL NEEDS
English Language Learners

Discuss the meaning of *dive* and *swim* by asking children to mime the actions. Review colors by playing a matching game using pictures of differently colored fish and color word cards.

Sharing the Big Book
Oral Language/Comprehension

▶ **Building Background**

Ask children to tell what they know about fish. Encourage them to include observations made from watching fish in a fish tank, at an aquarium, or in a lake, pond, or ocean. Then introduce the book *In the Big Blue Sea*.

Strategy: Summarize

Teacher Modeling Remind children that good readers remember important story parts to retell a story and help them understand it better. Model the Summarize strategy.

Think Aloud

I can tell from the title and from the picture that this book tells about real things found in the ocean. When I read a book about real things, I pay attention to information I can retell or share after reading. As I read, you think about this, too.

✓ Comprehension Focus:
Inferences: Making Predictions

Teacher Modeling Review that good readers predict what a book will be about before they read.

Think Aloud

I wonder what In the Big Blue Sea *is about. The title mentions the big blue sea and the picture shows real fish. I think the story tells about real things in the sea. As I look at the first few pictures, I think that I may be right. The pictures show real people and more fish.*

▶ Sharing the Story

Read the selection aloud, tracking the print as you read. Pause for children to study the beautiful photographs and comment on the fish.

▶ Responding

Personal Response Encourage children to use the language of the story as they react to it.

■ *How are the fish in the story alike? How are they different?*

■ *Which fish is your favorite? Why?*

At Group Time
Science Center

> **Materials** • nonfiction picture books about fish • mural paper
> • water colors • Blackline Master 37–38 • crayons

Have children create a class mural about fish. Children can paint the background with water colors. Then, using **Blackline Masters 37–38** as a guide, have them color or paint fish to add to the mural. Some children may want to refer to *In the Big Blue Sea* or other picture books to help them draw or label specific fish.

 Extra Support

Some children may not be familiar with the special equipment used to snorkel or dive underwater. Preview the pictures to identify the equipment and explain their uses.

OBJECTIVES

Children

• identify words that begin with /m/

• identify pictures whose names start with the letters *m, s*

• form the letters *Mm*

MATERIALS

• **Alphafriend Card** *Mimi Mouse*

• **Letter Cards** *m, s*

• **Picture Cards** *man, map, mop, sandbox, sandwich, six*

• **Blackline Master 00**

• **Phonics Center:** Theme 2, Week 2, Day 2

Extra Support

To help children remember the sound for *m*, point out that the letter's name gives a clue to its sound: *m, /m/.*

Phonics

✓ Initial Consonant m

▶ **Develop Phonemic Awareness**

Beginning Sound Read the lyrics to Mimi Mouse's song and have children echo it line-for-line. Have them listen for the /m/ words and point to their mouths each time they hear one.

Mimi Mouse's Song
(Tune: "This Old Man")

Mimi Mouse, Mimi Mouse,
Minds her manners in the house.
When she sips her milk,
　　she never makes a mess.
Mud pies never stain
　　her dress.

▶ **Connect Sounds to Letters**

Beginning Letter Display the *Mimi Mouse* card, and have children name the letter on the picture. Say: *The letter* m *stands for the sound /m/, as in* mouse. *When you see an* m, *remember Mimi Mouse. That will help you remember the sound /m/.*

Write *mouse* on the board, underlining the *m*. **What is the first letter in the word mouse?** (*m*) **Mouse** *starts with /m/, so* m *is the first letter I write for* mouse.

Compare and Review: s In a pocket chart, display the *Mimi Mouse* card with the Letter Card *m* below it. Place the Letter Card *s* next to the *m*. Display the Picture Cards in random order. Children can name a picture, say the beginning sound and letter, and then put the card either below the *m* or the *s*.

Pictures: *man, map, mop, sandbox, sandwich, six*

Tell children they will sort more pictures in the Phonics Center today.

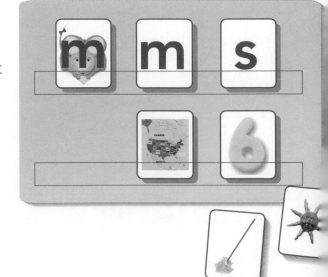

▶ Handwriting

Writing _M, m_ Tell children that now they'll learn to write the letters that stand for / m /: capital _M_ and small _m._ Write each letter as you recite the handwriting rhyme. Children can chant each rhyme as they "write" the letter in the air.

Handwriting Rhyme: M
Make a line going down.
Then two lines that meet.
One more, you're done.
It's very neat.

Handwriting Rhyme: m
Little _m_ is short.
Start in the middle.
Make two little hills.
It's not a riddle.

▶ Apply

Practice Book page 59 Children will complete this page at small group time.

Blackline Master 169 This page provides additional handwriting practice.

At Group Time

Phonics Center

Use the Phonics Center materials for **Theme 2, Week 2, Day 2.**

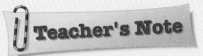
Practice Book p. 59

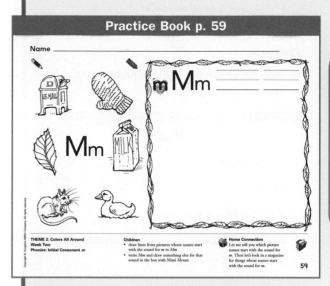

Teacher's Note

Handwriting practice for the continuous stroke style is available on **Blackline Master 195.**

Portfolio Opportunity
Save the Practice Book page to show children's grasp of the letter-sound association.
Save the **Blackline Master 169** for a handwriting sample.

OBJECTIVES

Children

- read and write the high-frequency word *see*

MATERIALS

- **Word Cards** *I, see*
- **Picture Cards** *berries, jam, toast*
- **Punctuation Card:** period
- ***Higglety Pigglety: A Book of Rhymes,*** page 44

✓ High-Frequency Word

New Word: see

▶ Teach

Tell children that today they will learn to read and write the word *see,* a word often used in stories. Say *see* and use it in context.

I *see* our classroom.　　　I can *see* you.　　　Can you *see* me?

Write *see* on the board, and have children spell it as you point to each letter. **Spell** *see* **with me, s-e-e.** Then lead children in a chant, clapping on each beat, to help them remember how *see* is spelled: **s-e-e, see! s-e-e, see.**

Word Wall Ask children to help you decide where on the Word Wall *see* should be posted. As needed, prompt children by pointing out that *see* begins with the letter *s.* When children find the letter *s* on the Word Wall, add *see* under it. Remind children to look there when they need to remember how to write the word.

▶ Practice

Reading Build the following sentences in a pocket chart. Have children take turns reading the sentences aloud. Leave the pocket chart so that children can practice building and reading sentences.

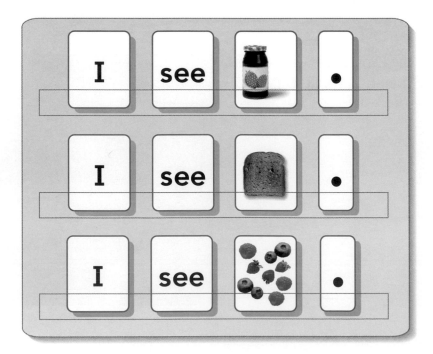

Display *Higglety Pigglety: A Book of Rhymes,* page 44.

■ Share the poem "Rhyme" aloud.

■ Reread the poem, asking children to listen for the word *see. I'll read the poem one more time. This time, listen for the word see. If you hear the word see raise your hand.*

■ Call on children to point to the word *see* each time it appears in the poem.

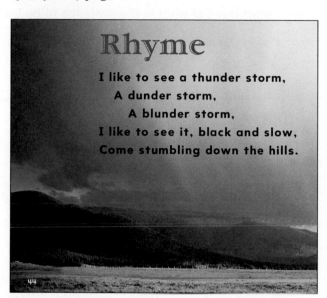

Rhyme

I like to see a thunder storm,
A dunder storm,
A blunder storm,
I like to see it, black and slow,
Come stumbling down the hills.

44

Higglety Pigglety: A Book of Rhymes, page 44

▶ Apply

Practice Book page 60 Children will read and write *see* as they complete the Practice Book page.

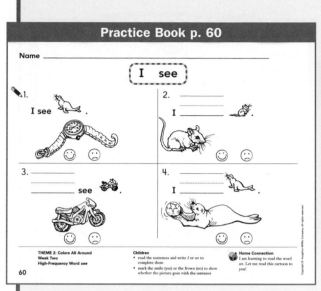

Practice Book p. 60

Diagnostic Check

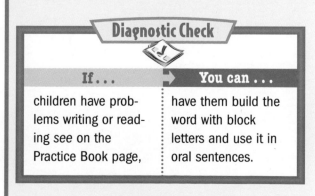

If . . .	You can . . .
children have problems writing or reading *see* on the Practice Book page,	have them build the word with block letters and use it in oral sentences.

Word Work
Day 2

OBJECTIVES

Children

- read high-frequency words
- create and write sentences with high-frequency words

MATERIALS

- **Word Cards** *I, see*
- **Picture Cards** color words; *berries, ink, jam, sandals, toast, toys, watermelon*
- **Punctuation Card:** period

High-Frequency Word Practice

▶ **Building Sentences**

Tell children that you want them to help build sentences.

■ Display the Picture and Word Cards in random order at the bottom of a pocket chart. Review the words together.

■ *I want the first word in the sentence to be* I. *Who can find that word?*

■ *I want the next word to be* see. Ask a volunteer to add the word *see* to the pocket chart.

■ Then have a child add the Picture Card *red* to the pocket chart. Together read: *I see red* _____.

■ *How could we finish the sentence?* Invite a volunteer to select a Picture Card to complete the sentence.

■ Read the sentence together, and then continue building other sentences.

Writing Opportunity Have children copy the sentence stem and choose a color word. Then have children complete the sentence by drawing a picture of something that is that color. Some children may refer to the Color Chart to write the color word.

Vocabulary Expansion

▶ Using Exact Naming Words

Viewing and Speaking Ask children to recall the Big Book *In the Big Blue Sea.* Point out that the word *fish* is a naming word. Page through the book and have children describe some of the fish.

- Remind children that some nouns are more exact than others. Display pages 18–19 of *In the Big Blue Sea* and read the names of the fish for children.

- Tell children that these words more clearly name the fish in the book.

- Allow children time to match a few of the fish on pages 18–19 to the fish in the selection. Ask, for example: **Which words more clearly name the fish on page 4, green fish** *or* **queen angelfish?**

OBJECTIVES

Children
- use exact words for fish

MATERIALS
- **Big Book:** *In the Big Blue Sea*

DAY 2

At Group Time

Book Center

Materials • Big Book: *In the Big Blue Sea*

Pairs of children can compare other fish in the glossary to those in the big book. One child can point to a specific fish, and the child's partner can locate it in the book. Together they can make a list of the fish they locate.

Day 3

Day at a Glance

Learning to Read

Big Book:

In the Big Blue Sea

☑ **Phonics:** Initial Consonant *m*, *page T88*

Word Work

Exploring Words, *page T90*

Writing & Language

Shared Writing, *page T91*

 Half-Day Kindergarten

☑ Indicates lessons for tested skills. Choose additional activities as time allows.

Opening

Calendar

Sunday	Monday	Tuesday	Wednesday	Thursday	Friday	Saturday
			1	2	3	4
5	6	7	8	9	10	11
12	13	14	15	16	17	18
19	20	21	22	23	24	25
26	27	28	29	30	31	

After completing the calendar routine, explore the colors in the classroom. *What green things can you see in the classroom? Is anyone wearing a green shirt? Is it a light or dark shade of green?*

Daily Message

Modeled Writing Talk about the color of the day. Use some of your morning discussion in the message. Call on children to name known letters. See the sample message.

> Good morning!
> Paul made us a
> green snack. Rikki
> brought green juice.

Ask children if they can find the new word they added to the Word Wall yesterday. Call on a volunteer to point it out. Have children chant the spelling of the word: **s-e-e** *spells* **see**. Then have children find and spell *I*: *capital* **I** *spells* **I**.

Daily Phonemic Awareness
Beginning Sounds

- Display Picture Cards for: *boat, bug, desk, dog, hen, hose, lamp, leash.* Name each picture with children.

- Play a beginning sound game. Hold up Picture Card *boat*. **Say boat with me. Listen as I name the other pictures. Raise your hand when you hear a word that begins with the same beginning sound as boat.** When most hands are up, have children name the picture that begins like *boat*. (bug) Continue with the other Picture Cards.

Syllables in Spoken Words

- Read aloud "Rhyme" on page 44 of *Higglety Pigglety*.

- I will say a word from the poem, and you clap the word parts. **Listen: thunder.** Clap the word parts with me: *thun-der*. **How may claps did you hear? Yes, two!**

- Continue with these words from the poem: *wonder, loudly, window.*

Getting Ready to Learn

To help plan their day, tell children that they will

- reread and talk about the Big Book: *In the Big Blue Sea.*

- read a story called "Look at Me."

- make a fish mobile in the Art Center.

Day 3

Sharing the Big Book

Children

- make predictions
- recognize use of capital letter at the beginning of a sentence
- recognize use of end punctuation: period, question mark

Big Book

In the Big Blue Sea

by Chyng Feng Sun
Photography by Norbert Wu

Includes:
Science Link

Reading for Understanding Reread the story, emphasizing the rhyme, rhythm, and the color words. Pause for discussion points.

 Extra Support
MEETING INDIVIDUAL NEEDS

If children have trouble naming the colors in the fish, have them practice matching color swatches and naming the colors with a partner.

I will swim in the big blue sea!
Come along and swim with me.

1

page 1

What color fish will you see?　2

What color fish would you like to be?　3

pages 2–3

Dive and swim,
splish, *splash*, splish!
Would you be a green fish?
4

Dive and swim,
splish, *splash*, splish!
Would you be a red fish?
5

pages 4–5

Dive and swim,
splish, *splash*, splish!
Would you be a yellow fish?

6

Dive and swim,
splish, *splash*, splish!
Would you be an orange fish?

7

pages 6–7

What color fish will you see?

8

What color fish would you like to be?

9

pages 8–9

Dive and swim,
splish, *splash*, splish!
Would you be a white fish?

10

Dive and swim,
splish, *splash*, splish!
Would you be a blue fish?

11

pages 10–11

▶ **Supporting Comprehension**

page 1

Noting Details

■ *The man on this page is Norbert Wu. He took the pictures for this story. What things does Norbert Wu use to take his underwater pictures?*

pages 2–3

✓ **Comprehension Focus: Inferences: Making Predictions**

Teacher-Student Modeling Read aloud the text on pages 2–3. Have children use the questions to predict what fish they will read about on the following pages. *What color fish will you see?*

pages 4–7

Strategy: Summarize

Teacher-Student Modeling Remind children that good readers think about the important information in a story to remember the story and tell about it later. Prompts: *What kind of fish have we read about so far?* (green, red, yellow, orange)

pages 8–9

Compare and Contrast

■ *How are the fish on these pages alike? How are they different?*

DAY 3

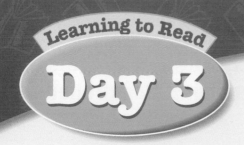

Learning to Read
Day 3

Dive and swim,
splish, *splash*, splish!
Would you be a purple fish?

12

Dive and swim,
splish, *splash*, splish!
Would you be a black fish?

13

pages 12–13

▶ **Supporting Comprehension**

pages 16–17

Strategy: Summarize

Student Modeling *What does Norbert Wu do? What are some of the fish he took pictures of?*

Revisiting the Text

pages 14–16

Concept of Print

 Capitalize First Word in Sentence; End Punctuation

- Read the sentence on page 14. Frame *What.* **Why does** What *begin with a capital letter?*

- *What kind of sentence is this? How do you know?* (asking sentence; asks question, ends with a question mark)

- Repeat with the sentence on page 16. Have children note the use of a capital letter to begin the sentence and identify the end mark as a period.

What color fish did you see?

14

What color fish would you like to be?

15

pages 14–15

We swam like fish in the big blue sea.

16

I'm so glad you swam with me!

17

pages 16–17

NAME: Queen Angelfish
HABITAT: Caribbean

NAME: Blue Spotted Grouper
HABITAT: Indo-Pacific

NAME: Redback Butterflyfish
HABITAT: Red Sea

NAME: Powder Blue Surgeonfish
HABITAT: Indo-Pacific

NAME: Three-spotted Angelfish
HABITAT: Indo-Pacific

NAME: Clownfish
HABITAT: Indo-Malaysian Archipelago to Japan

NAME: Blackcap Basslet
HABITAT: Bahamas, northwestern and southern Caribbean

NAME: Juvenile French Angelfish
HABITAT: Caribbean

18   19

pages 18–19

▶ Supporting Comprehension

Teacher's Note

Discuss with children how these pages are different from the other pages in the selection. Explain
that books that tell about real things sometimes
have a special book part called a *glossary*. The
glossary tells more about the things in the book.

pages 2–19

✔ Comprehension Focus: Inferences: Making Predictions

Student Modeling Have children browse through
the book and point out places where they were to
able predict what they would see or read about
next. Ask children to tell what clues they used to
make their predictions.

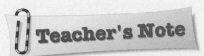
Teacher's Note

Language Patterns On a rereading, point out
the words *splish* and *splash*. Explain that some
words sound like the sounds that they stand for.
Cite other examples, such as *thud, tick-tock,* and
boom.

English Language Learners

Distribute the color Picture Cards to partners. Have
partners browse through the book and match the
cards to the colors in the story.

DAY 3

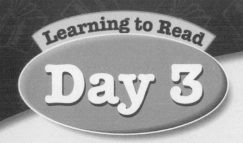

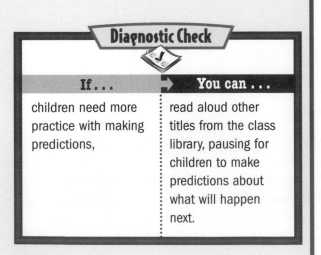

▶ ## Responding to the Story

Retelling Use prompts to help children summarize the selection:

- *What did Norbert Wu do at the beginning of the book?*

- *What fish did Norbert Wu and the children see?*

- *How do color words help you to remember the kinds of fish you saw?*

Practice Book page 61 Children will complete the page at small group time.

Literature Circle Have small groups discuss what might happen if the book were to continue. *What other fish might Norbert Wu see? What color would these fish be?*

Diagnostic Check

If . . .	You can . . .
children need more practice with making predictions,	read aloud other titles from the class library, pausing for children to make predictions about what will happen next.

Materials • Blackline Masters 37–38 • paints and brushes
• crayons or markers • string • coat hangers

Use **Blackline Masters 37–38** to prepare fish shapes that resemble
the fish in *In the Big Blue Sea*. Display pages 18–19 of the Big Book
in the Art Center. Ask children to match the fish shapes to the fish
on the glossary page and paint the fish accordingly. Then hang the
fish from varying lengths of string from the hangers to create fish
mobiles.

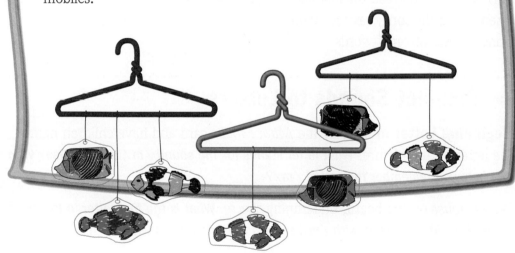

DAY 3

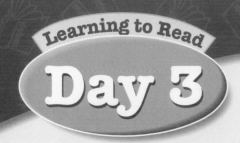
Phonics

✓ Initial Consonant m

▶ Develop Phonemic Awareness

Beginning Sound Read the lyrics to Mimi Mouse's song aloud, and have children echo it line-for-line. Have them listen for the /m/ words.

Read the song again. *This time, if you hear a word that begins with /m/ stand up. If you hear another /m/ word, sit back down. We'll do this each time we hear an /m/ word.* As needed, model standing and sitting alternately for /m/ words as you read the first line. Then reread the song, having children stand and sit for /m/ words.

> ### Mimi Mouse's Song
> (Tune: "This Old Man")
>
> Mimi Mouse, Mimi Mouse,
> Minds her manners in the house.
> When she sips her milk,
>   she never makes a mess.
> Mud pies never stain
>   her dress.

▶ Connect Sounds to Letters

Beginning Letter *m* Display the *Mimi Mouse* card and have children name the letter on the picture. *What letter stands for the sound /m/, as in* mouse? *Who can help you remember the sound /m/?*

Write *mouse* on the board, underlining the *m*. *What is the first letter in the word* mouse? (m) Mouse *starts with /m/, so m is the first letter I write for* mouse.

Compare and Review Write *Mm* on the board and circle it. Then write *Mm,* circle it, and draw a line through it to represent "not *m*." Distribute Picture Cards for *m* and assorted other Picture Cards, one to a child, to a small group of children. In turn, children name the picture, say the beginning sound, and stand below the correct symbol on the board. Children without Picture Cards verify their decisions.

Repeat the activity with different groups of children until each child has a chance to name a picture, say the beginning sound, and stand below the correct symbol on the board.

OBJECTIVES

Children
- identify words that begin with /m/
- identify pictures whose names start with the letter *m*

MATERIALS

- **Alphafriend Card** *Mimi Mouse*
- **Alphafriend Audiotape** Theme 2
- **Picture Cards** for *m* and assorted others

MEETING INDIVIDUAL NEEDS

Extra Support

Read "I Went Upstairs," on page 12 of *Higglety Pigglety*. Have children touch a finger to their mouths each time they hear a word that begins with /m/. Then call on volunteers to point to words that begin with *m* in the rhyme.

Applying Skills

▶ Introducing the Story

Let's look at the title page. The title is "Look at Me." I see face paints in the picture. What do you think we'll see?

Together identify pictures that begin with the /m/ sound on the title page.

Let's look at the pictures. Looking at the pictures is a good way to tell what a story will be about. As you do a picture walk, guide children in a discussion of the pictures.

▶ Coached Reading

Have children look carefully at each page before discussing it with you. Prompts:

page 10   *This little girl is having her nose painted. What color is her nose going to be when it is painted?*

page 12   *What is the face painter painting on the boy's face?*

page 13   *All of the children's faces are painted. Who do you think painted their faces?*

pages 14–15 *Who is the face painter? Why do you think this person is so good at painting faces?*

Now let's go back and look at each page to find things that begin with Mimi Mouse's sound m-m-m.

Phonics Library

Purposes
- read a wordless story
- find pictures beginning with /m/

Look at Me!
by Susan Gorman-Howe
illustrated by Jennifer Plecas

FACE PAINTING

9

10   11

12   13

14   15

 Home Connection

Children can color the pictures in the take-home version of "Look at Me." After rereading on Day 4, children can take it home to read to family members.

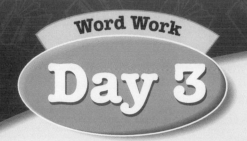

Exploring Words

▶ Color Words

Ask children to look at the picture of the man with his caps as you read *Caps of Many Colors*. Then reread the second paragraph, which describes the color of the caps, aloud.

Reread the last sentence of the paragraph: ***Crowning the whole stack were caps in every shade of red you could imagine, from strawberry to scarlet.***

■ Begin a discussion of shades of color with children. Use words like *bright, light,* and *dark.* Define *strawberry red* as a deep, dark red and *scarlet* as a bright, fiery red.

■ Repeat the expression *strawberry red.* Mention to children that when people want you to have a clear idea of a color they are talking about, they may compare it to something else. Ask children if they have ever heard of colors like *sky blue, lemon yellow,* and *lime green*.

■ Point to various items in the classroom and ask children to describe the color of the item by comparing it to something else. List their suggestions on chart paper, organizing the phrases by color.

 Writing Opportunity Have children choose one of the color phrases from the chart to illustrate. Label the drawings for children.

banana yellow

apple red

Shared Writing

▶ Writing a Description

Viewing and Speaking Display the fish mobiles children made in the Art Center today. Tell children that they are going to describe the different types of fish that they see. Remind children to look for patterns or shades of color on the fish to help them with their descriptions.

Begin by pointing to a fish and describing it. Say: *I see a fire-engine red fish. What do you see?* Then hand a small beanbag to a child to show that it is his or her turn. As children descibe the fish, record their answers on chart paper.

> I see a ____ fish.
> What do you see?
>
> fire engine red
> grape purple
> sunny yellow.

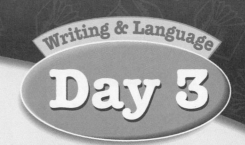

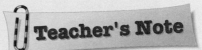
Teacher's Note

It may be necessary to prompt some children to complete their descriptions. Ask: *Is the fish a bright color? a pale color? Does the fish have spots?*

DAY 3

Day at a Glance

Learning to Read

Big Book:

What Do You Do, Norbert Wu?

✓ **Phonics: Initial Consonant / m /,** *page T96*

Word Work

Exploring Words, *page T98*

Writing & Language

Interactive Writing, *page T99*

 Half-Day Kindergarten

✓ Indicates lessons for tested skills. Choose additional activities as time allows.

Opening

Calendar

Sunday	Monday	Tuesday	Wednesday	Thursday	Friday	Saturday
			1	2	3	4
5	6	7	8	9	10	11
12	13	14	15	16	17	18
19	20	21	22	23	24	25
26	27	28	29	30	31	

Have a volunteer find today's date on the calendar. Then ask questions about the month. *How many days have there been since the first day of the month? How many days are there until the end of the month?*

Daily Message

Modeled Writing Use some words that begin with *m* in today's message. Have children circle the *m*'s they see.

This morning, we will measure ourselves in the Math Center.

Word Wall

Have children recite the alphabet with you. Then ask children to find and read the words that they've added to the Word Wall. Ask children to tell why the words are under the letters that they are.

Routines

 ## Daily Phonemic Awareness
Beginning Sounds

- *Listen as I say two words:* food, fish. *Say the words with me:* food, fish. *Do you hear the same sound at the beginning of each word? Yes,* food *and* fish *begin with the same sound.*

- Play a listening game with children. *I will say two words. You listen carefully and tell me the same beginning sound,/ f /.* Say the pairs of words shown.

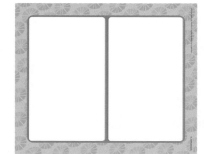

book/ball	lake/leaf
duck/dog	pot/peach
cap/comb	toad/tail
car/cake	key/king
house/hat	

☑ Syllables in Spoken Words

- *Today, we'll clap the word parts we hear in fish names. Listen:* clown-fish.

- Say *clownfish* again, clapping the syllables. *How may claps did you hear? Yes, two! Now say and clap the word with me:* clownfish.

- Continue with other fish names from *In the Big Blue Sea.*

Getting Ready to Learn

To help plan their day, tell children that they will

- read the Science Link: *What Do You Do, Norbert Wu?*

- sort *m* words in the Phonics Center.

- reread a book called "Look at Me."

DAY 4

Day 4

OBJECTIVES

Children

- make predictions

- recognize use of capital letter at the beginning of a sentence

- recognize use of end punctuation: period, question mark

Big Book

What Do You Do, Norbert Wu?

In the Big Blue Sea
by Chyng Feng Sun,
Photography by Norbert Wu

pages 21–26

English Language Learners

Discuss photography with children. Say the word and have children say it with you. Mention that when people take photographs they usually say *take pictures.* You may also wish to introduce underwater vocabulary: *diver, scuba diving, oxygen tank, underwater camera, flash.*

Sharing the Big Book
Science Link

▶ Building Background

Ask children to tell if they know the name of someone who takes pictures. Then have them talk about photographs they have seen or have taken. Read aloud the title and discuss the cover. Recall that Norbert Wu took the photographs for *In the Big Blue Sea.* **Which picture shows Norbert Wu underwater? Which picture shows him out of the water?**

Reading for Understanding Pause for discussion as you share the selection.

---

page 21

Strategy: Summarize

Student Modeling Remind children that they have to listen for important information in order to summarize or tell about a selection. Ask: *What will you look for as we read the story?*

Comprehension Focus: Inferences: Making Predictions

Student Modeling Remind children that good readers make predictions about a story and check their predictions as they read. Ask: *How can the pictures on the title page help you predict what Norbert Wu does? How can you check your predictions?*

---

page 22

Noting Details

■ *What does a photographer do? What kind of photographer is Norbert Wu?*

pages 24–25

Drawing Conclusions

■ *Why do you think Norbert Wu also takes pictures of starfish and seals?*

page 26

Compare and Contrast

■ *How are these fish the same? Different?*

I am a photographer.
I take pictures.

22

I see a shark!
Click!

23

pages 22–23

I see a starfish!
Click!

24

I see seals!
Click!

25

pages 24–25

I took these pictures of fish.
Can you find them in this book?

26

page 26

page 26

Concepts of Print

☑ **Capitalize First Word in Sentence;
End Punctuation**

■ Frame and read *I took these pictures of fish.*
**What kind of sentence is this? How can you
tell?** (telling sentence; ends with period.)

■ Frame and read *Can you find them in this
book?* **Why does the word** Can **begin with a
capital letter?** (It is the first word in the sentence.)
**What kind of sentence is this? How can you
tell?** (asking sentence; question mark)

▶ Responding

Summarizing Have children respond to the title
question to summarize the selection.

Oral Language

click The sound a camera makes when you push
the button to take a picture. Click is a word that
stands for the sound it makes.

DAY 4

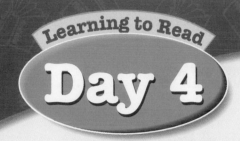
MATERIALS

• **Alphafriend Cards** *Mimi Mouse, Sammy Seal*

• **Alphafolder** *Mimi Mouse*

• **Letter Cards** *m, s*

• **Picture Cards** *man, map, mix, mule, salt, seal, six, sun*

• ***From Apples to Zebras: A Book of ABCs,*** page 14

• **Phonics Center:** Theme 2, Week 2, Day 4

Home Connection

Challenge children to look at home for items or for names that begin with the consonant *m*. Children can draw pictures to show what they have found.

Phonics

Review Initial Consonant m

▶ Develop Phonemic Awareness

Beginning Sound Display the scene in Mimi Mouse's Alphafolder. *One thing I see in Mimi's kitchen is a mop. Say* mop *with me. Does* mop *begin with the same sound as Mimi Mouse, / m /?* Call on volunteers to point to and name other items in the picture that begin with / m /.

▶ Connect Sounds to Letters

Review Consonant *m* Using self-stick notes, cover the words on page 14 of *From Apples to Zebras: A Book of ABC's.* Then display the page. Ask children what letter they expect to see first in each word and why. (*m*; words begin with / m /) Uncover the words so that children can check their predictions.

From Apples to Zebras: A Book of ABC's, page 14

▶ Apply

Compare and Review: *m, s* In a pocket chart, display the cards for *Mimi Mouse* and *Sammy Seal* as well as the Letter Cards *m* and *s*. Review the sound for *m*, / m / and *s*, / s /.

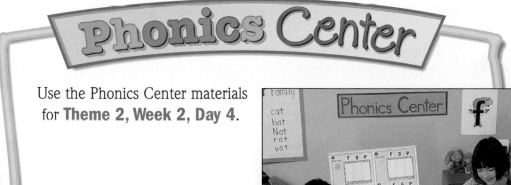

Hold up Picture Cards one at a time. Have children name a picture, say the beginning sound, and place the card below the correct letter.

Pictures: *seal, map, six, mule, salt, mix, sun, man*

Tell children they will sort more pictures in the Phonics Center today.

Practice Book page 62 Children will complete this page at small group time.

Phonics Library In groups today, children will also identify pictures that begin with / m / as they reread the **Phonics Library** story "Look at Me." See suggestions, page T89.

Phonics Center

Use the Phonics Center materials for **Theme 2, Week 2, Day 4**.

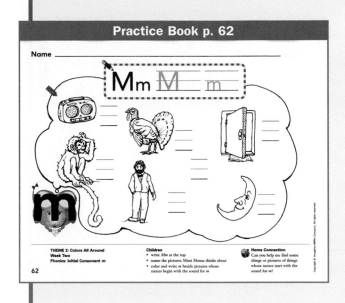
DAY 4

Diagnostic Check

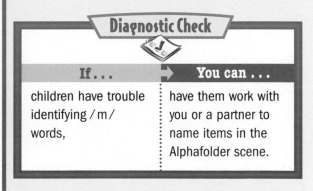

If . . .	You can . . .
children have trouble identifying / m / words,	have them work with you or a partner to name items in the Alphafolder scene.

Phonics (T97)

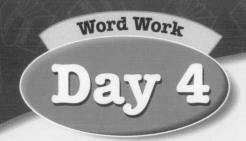
Exploring Words

▶ Color Words

Display the chart children used during yesterday's Word Work activity. Read through the chart with children.

■ Recall with children that in *Caps of Many Colors,* the peddler had caps in many shades of red, from strawberry to scarlet. Explain to children that some color words, like *strawberry red,* use common things to help describe how light, dark, or bright they are. Other color words, like *scarlet,* are special color words use to name a shade of color

■ Brainstorm other color words with children. You may want to read the color words on some crayons.

■ Add any new color words to the chart.

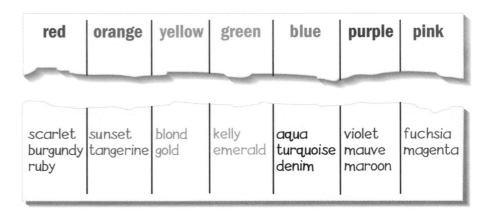

red	orange	yellow	green	blue	purple	pink
scarlet burgundy ruby	sunset tangerine	blond gold	kelly emerald	aqua turquoise denim	violet mauve maroon	fuchsia magenta

✏ **Writing Opportunity** Have children draw pictures of themselves wearing favorite clothes. Children can label their drawings with color words. Encourage children to choose color words that will help people know just what shade of color they are talking about.

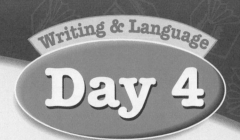
Interactive Writing

▶ Writing a Description

Display and read the chart from yesterday's shared writing activity.

- Have children write a story about the colorful fish listed on the chart or the fish Norbert Wu photographed for his book.

- Ask them to write the beginning consonants *s* and *m*. They can also add the appropriate end punctuation.

Many Fish in the Sea

We saw 5 striped fish.
One was purple and green.
Two more were orange and white.
Another two were scarlet
    and pale blue.
They swam away from the
    big sunny yellow fish.

DAY 4

Day 5

Day at a Glance

Learning to Read

Revisiting the Literature:

Caps of Many Colors, In the Big Blue Sea, What Do You Do, Norbert Wu?, "Look at Me"

☑ **Phonics: Initial Consonant** *m*, *page T104*

Word Work

Exploring Words, *page T106*

Writing & Language

Independent Writing, *page T107*

 Half-Day Kindergarten

☑ Indicates lessons for tested skills. Choose additional activities as time allows.

Opening

Calendar

Sunday	Monday	Tuesday	Wednesday	Thursday	Friday	Saturday
			1	2	3	4
5	6	7	8	9	10	11
12	13	14	15	16	17	18
19	20	21	22	23	24	25
26	27	28	29	30	31	

As children share the colored items they've worn today, encourage them to use color words that more clearly define the shade of their clothing.

Daily Message

Interactive Writing Have children help you write the daily message. *What kind of letter should I use to begin my sentence?... How should I end each sentence, with a period or a question mark?*

> Ms. Sullivan's favorite color is blue. What is your favorite color?

Read the Word Wall together, and then play a rhyming game: *Find a word on the wall that rhymes with* my... *Yes,* I *rhymes with* my. *Find a word on the wall that rhymes with* tree... *Yes,* see *rhymes with* tree.

✓ Daily Phonemic Awareness
Beginning Sounds

- Secretly choose a child's name. Say: *I am thinking of someone who has a name that starts with /m/?*

- Allow children to guess all the possibilities before revealing the name.

- Repeat several times, letting children take turns thinking of names.

✓ Syllables in Spoken Words

- Remind children that they have been clapping the number of parts they hear in words.

- Choose the names of common classroom items. Say each word, for example: *ta-ble.* Then children say the word and clap the word parts.

- Continue with the names of other classroom items.

Getting Ready to Learn

To help plan their day, tell children that they will

- reread and talk about all the books they've read this week.

- take home a story they can read.

- write about a career choice in their journals.

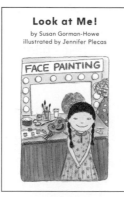

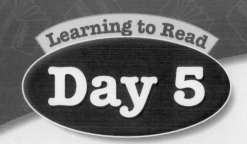

Day 5

Revisiting the Literature

....

▶ Literature Discussion

Today children will compare the different books you shared this week: *Caps of Many Colors*, *In the Big Blue Sea*, *What Do You Do, Norbert Wu?* and "Look at Me." Use these suggestions to help children recall the selections:

■ Have children retell *Caps of Many Colors* in their own words. Ask how the man was able to get his caps back from the monkeys.

■ Display *In the Big Blue Sea*. Have children describe the fish they read about.

■ Call on volunteers to answer the question *What Do You Do, Norbert Wu?* Allow children to tell if they would like a job like Norbert Wu's.

■ Together, read "Look at Me." Ask volunteers to name the / m / pictures in the story.

■ Ask children to vote for their favorite book of the week. Then read the text of the winner aloud.

✓ Comprehension Focus: Making Predictions

Comparing Books Remind children that good readers predict what a book is about before reading and predict what will happen next while reading. Browse through each story, asking how children were able to make predictions. For example, language patterns and picture clues helped children to predict the monkeys' actions in *Caps of Many Colors* and what fish would appear in *In the Big Blue Sea*. Prior knowledge of Norbert Wu's work, along with picture clues, helped them to predict the answer to the title question *What Do You Do, Norbert Wu?* After looking at each selection, help children develop a one- or two-sentence summary of it.

Technology

www.eduplace.com

Log on to **Education Place** for more activities relating to Colors All Around.

www.bookadventure.org

This Internet reading-incentive program provides thousands of titles for children to read.

Building Fluency

▶ Rereading Familiar Texts

Phonics Library: "Look at Me" Remind children that they've learned the new word *see*, and that they've been learning about words with initial *m*. As they reread the **Phonics Library** story "Look at Me" have them look for /m/ pictures.

Review Feature several familiar **Phonics Library** titles in the Book Corner. Have children demonstrate their growing skills by choosing one to reread aloud, alternating pages with a partner. From time to time ask children to point out words or pages that they can read more easily now.

Oral Reading Frequent rereadings of familiar texts help children develop a less word-by word and more expressive style in their oral reading. Model often how to read in phrases, pausing for end punctuation. Then have children try it.

Look at Me!
by Susan Gorman-Howe
illustrated by Jennifer Plecas

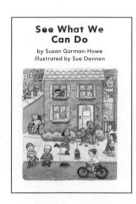

See What We Can Do
by Susan Gorman-Howe
illustrated by Sue Dennen

We Can Make It
by Susan Gorman-Howe
illustrated by Anthony Lewis

Blackline Master 36 Children complete the page and take it home to share their reading progress.

My Reading Log

I can read

My new words

see

Leveled Books

The materials listed below provide reading practice for children at different levels.

Little Big Books

Little Readers for Guided Reading

Houghton Mifflin Classroom Bookshelf

Home Connection

Remind children to share the **take-home version** of "Look at Me" with their families.

DAY 5

Phonics Review

✓ Initial Consonants: m, s

▶ Review

Tell children that they will take turns naming pictures and telling what letter stands for the beginning sound.

■ Randomly place four Picture Cards, along the chalkboard ledge and write *m* and *s* on the board. Call on four children to come up and stand in front of a Picture Card. In turn, have each child name the picture, say the initial sound, and point to *m* or *s*.

■ Have the rest of the class verify that the correct letter has been chosen and pointed to. Then write the picture name on the board and underline the initial consonant.

■ Continue until everyone has a chance to name a picture and point to the consonant that stands for its beginning sound.

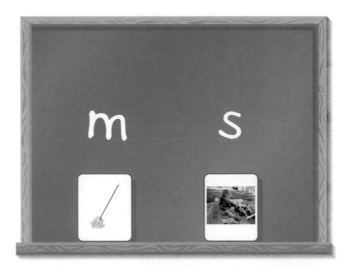

High-Frequency Word Review
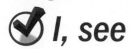 *I, see*

▶ Review

Give each small group the Word Cards, Picture Cards, and Punctuation Card needed to make a sentence. Each child holds one card. Children stand and arrange themselves to make a sentence for others to read.

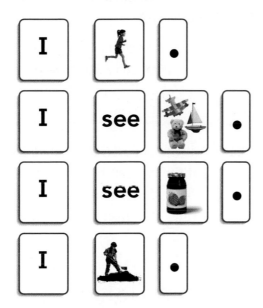

▶ Apply

Practice Book page 63 Children can complete this page independently and read it to you during small group time.

Phonics Library Have children take turns reading aloud to the class. Each child might read one page of "Look at Me" or a favorite **Phonics Library** selection. Remind readers to share the pictures!

Questions for discussion:

■ *Can you find any pictures that start with the same sound as Mimi Mouse's name? What is the letter? What is the sound?*

■ *Are there any pictures in "Look at Me" that begin with Sammy Seal's sound?*

Practice Book p. 63

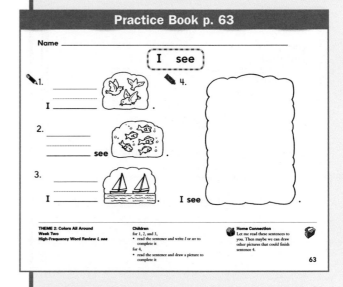

Portfolio Opportunity

Children may wish to add the Practice Book page to their portfolios as a sample of what they have learned.

Diagnostic Check

If...	You can ...
children need help remembering the sound for consonant *m*,	have them listen to Mimi Mouse's song and listen for *m* words.

DAY 5

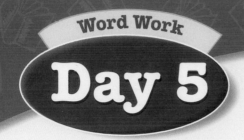

OBJECTIVES

Children
- explore color words

MATERIALS

- *From Apples to Zebras: A Book of ABC's*
- **Color Word Cards:** color words

Exploring Words

▶ **Color Words**

Display page 29 of *From Apples to Zebras: A Book of ABC's.* Call on volunteers to point to and name the colors on the page.

■ Then distribute the Word Cards. Call on volunteers to match the Word Cards to the color words on the page.

■ Discuss the colors with children. *What other words have you learned that help to name the color red? the color green?*

■ Have children recall the colors of the fish they read about in *In the Big Blue Sea.* *What fish colors surprised you? What color fish have you seen?*

Writing Opportunity Invite children to create a fish of their own design. Tell children that the fish can be any color they choose. The fish can also have stripes, spots, or other designs on them. Have children draw or paint their fish. When the drawings are finished, children can label the fish by color and create a name for it.

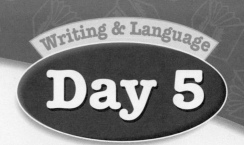
Independent Writing

Journals Direct attention to this week's shared and interactive writing posted in the classroom. Have volunteers read the writing samples. Point out the different color words children used. Tell children that today they will write in their journals about something they learned.

- Pass out the journals.

- *Let's discuss some of the things we read about this week. What did the man sell in* Caps of Many Colors? *What did Norbert Wu take pictures of in* In the Big Blue Sea? *What can you tell me about Norbert Wu's job?*

- Tell children that they will now have a chance to write about something they did this week. Children might write about their favorite fish in *In the Big Blue Sea* or write and draw about a picture they would like to take. As children write, remind them that they can use the words on the Word Wall and those posted in the Writing and Science Centers for help in writing words.

- If time permits, have children share what they've written with the class.

OBJECTIVES

Children
- write independently

MATERIALS

- journals

Portfolio Opportunity

Mark journal entries you would like to share with parents. Allow children to mark their best efforts or favorite works for sharing as well.

DAY 5

English Language Learners

Children may have difficulty writing by themselves. Have them work in small groups to create one descriptive sentence each, which can be copied into their journals.

Literature for Week 3

Different texts for different purposes

Teacher Read Aloud

- **I Need a Lunchbox**
- **Caps of Many Colors**
- **How the Birds Got Their Colors**

Purposes

- oral language
- listening strategy
- comprehension skill

Big Books: Main Selections

Purposes

- concepts of print
- reading strategy
- story language
- comprehension skills

Big Books

Higglety Piggglety: A Book of Rhymes

Purposes

- oral language development
- phonemic awareness

Also available in Little Big Book and audiotape

From Apples to Zebras: A Book of ABC's

Purposes

- alphabet recognition
- letters and sounds

Also available in Little Big Book and audiotape

Leveled Books

Also in the Big Books:
- Science Links

Purposes

- reading strategies
- comprehension skills
- concepts of print

Phonics Library

Also available in Take-Home version

Purpose

- applying phonics skills and high-frequency words

On My Way Paperback

Beautiful Butterflies
by Demaris Tyler
page T153

Little Readers for Guided Reading
Collection K

Houghton Mifflin Classroom Bookshelf
Level K

Technology

www.eduplace.com

Log on to *Education Place* for more activities relating to *Colors All Around*.

www.bookadventure.org

This free Internet reading incentive program provides thousands of titles for students to read.

Suggested Daily Routines

Instructional Goals

Learning to Read

✓ *Phonemic Awareness:* Beginning Sounds, Syllables in Spoken Words

Strategy Focus: Predict/Infer, Summarize

✓ *Comprehension Skill:* Sequence of Events, Inferences: Making Predictions

✓ *Phonics Skills*

Phonemic Awareness: Beginning Sound /r/

Initial Consonant *R, r*

Compare and Review: Initial Consonants: *m, s*

✓ *High-Frequency Review Words: I, see*

✓ *Concepts of Print:* Capital at Beginning of Sentence, End Punctuation

Word Work

High-Frequency Word Practice: Color Words

Writing & Language

Vocabulary Skills: Using Singular and Plural Words, Using Plural Names

Writing Skills: Writing a Graphic Organizer, Writing a Class Story

✓ = tested skills

 Leveled Books

Have children read in appropriate levels daily.

Phonics Library
On My Way Practice Readers
Little Big Books
Houghton Mifflin Classroom Bookshelf

Day 1

Opening Routines, *T114–T115*

Word Wall
- **Phonemic Awareness:** Beginning Sounds, Syllables in Spoken Words

Teacher Read Aloud
How the Birds Got Their Colors, T116–T119
- **Strategy:** Predict/Infer
- **Comprehension:** Sequence of Events

Phonics
Instruction
- Phonemic Awareness, Beginning Sound /r/, *T120–T121; Practice Book, 67–68*

High-Frequency Word Practice
- Words: *I, see, T122*

Oral Language
- Using Singular and Plural Words, *T123*
- Viewing and Speaking, *T123*

Managing Small Groups
Teacher-Led Group
- Reread familiar **Phonics Library** selections

Independent Groups
- Finish Practice Book, *65–68*
- *Phonics Center:* Theme 2, Week 3, Day 1
- Book, Dramatic Play, Writing, other Centers

Day 2

Opening Routines, *T124–T125*

Word Wall
- **Phonemic Awareness:** Beginning Sounds, Syllables in Spoken Words

Sharing the Big Book
I Went Walking, T126–T127
- **Strategy:** Predict/Infer
- **Comprehension:** Inferences: Making Predictions

Phonics
Instruction, Practice
- Initial Consonant *r, T128–T129*
- *Practice Book, 69*

High-Frequency Words
- Review Words: *I, see, T130–T131*

High-Frequency Word Practice
- Building Sentences, *T132*

Vocabulary Expansion
- Using Plural Names, *T133*
- Viewing and Speaking, *T33*

Managing Small Groups
Teacher-Led Group
- Begin *Practice Book, 69* and handwriting Blackline Masters 174 or 200.

Independent Groups
- Finish *Practice Book, 69* and handwriting Blackline Masters 174 or 200.
- *Phonics Center:* Theme 2, Week 3, Day 2
- Science, Art, other Centers

Technology

Lesson Planner CD-ROM: Customize your planning for *Colors All Around* with the Lesson Planner.

Day 3

Opening Routines, *T134–T135*

Word Wall
- **Phonemic Awareness:** Beginning Sounds, Syllables in Spoken Words

Sharing the Big Book
In the Big Blue Sea, T136–T137
- **Strategy:** Summarize
- **Comprehension:** Inferences: Making Predictions, *T136; Practice Book, 70*

Phonics

Practice, Application
- Initial Consonant *r, T138–T139*

Instruction
- Beginning Letter *r, T138–T139*
- **Phonics Library:** "The Parade," *T139*

Exploring Words
- Color Words, *T140*

✏️ **Shared Writing**
- Writing a Graphic Organizer, *T141*

Managing Small Groups
Teacher-Led Group
- Read **Phonics Library** selection "The Parade"
- Begin *Practice Book, 70*

Independent Groups
- Finish *Practice Book, 70*
- Science, other Centers

Day 4

Opening Routines, *T142–T143*

Word Wall
- **Phonemic Awareness:** Beginning Sounds, Syllables in Spoken Words

Sharing the Big Books
Science Links: "What's My Favorite Color?," *T144;* "What Do You Do, Norbert Wu?," *T145*
- **Strategy:** Summarize, Predict/Infer
- **Comprehension:** Sequence of Events; Inferences: Making Predictions
- **Concepts of Print:** Capital at Beginning of Sentence, End Punctuation

Phonics

Practice
- Review Initial Consonant *r, T146–T147; Practice Book, 71*

Exploring Words
- Color Words, *T148*

✏️ **Interactive Writing**
- Writing a Class Story, *T149*

Managing Small Groups
Teacher-Led Group
- Reread **Phonics Library** selection "The Parade"
- Begin *Practice Book, 71*

Independent Groups
- Finish *Practice Book, 71*
- *Phonics Center:* Theme 2, Week 3, Day 4
- Science, other Centers

Day 5

Opening Routines, *T150–T151*

Word Wall
- **Phonemic Awareness:** Beginning Sounds, Syllables in Spoken Words

Revisiting the Literature
Comprehension: Making Predictions, Sequence of Events, *T152*
Building Fluency
- **On My Way Practice Reader:** "Beautiful Butterflies," *T153*

Phonics

Review
- Initial Consonants: *r, m, s, T154*

High-Frequency Word Review
- Words: *I, see, T155; Practice Book, 72*

Exploring Words
- Color Words, *T156*

✏️ **Independent Writing**
- Journals: Favorite Color Activity, *T157*

Managing Small Groups
Teacher-Led Group
- Reread familiar **Phonics Library** selections
- Begin *Practice Book, 72,* **Blackline Master 36.**

Independent Groups
- Reread **Phonics Library** selections
- Finish *Practice Book, 72,* **Blackline Master 36.**
- Centers

Setting up the Centers

Teacher's Note

Gather the picture books about the sea early in the week for the Science Center.

bird

birds

Phonics Center

Materials • Phonics Center Kit materials for Theme 2, Week 3

Pairs work together to sort Picture Cards by beginning sound. See pages T121, T129, and T147 for this week's Phonics Center activities.

Writing Center

Materials • singular and plural words chart from Day 1

Children draw several pictures based on the chart. Then children use their knowledge of consonants and initial sounds to label their pictures. See page T123 for this week's Writing Center activity.

Dramatic Play Center

Materials • paper lunch bags • colored markers • colored paper

Children make bird paper bag puppets. Small groups can act out the Read Aloud story. See page T117 for this week's Dramatic Play Center.

Science Center

Materials • Blackline Masters 39–40 • animals picture books • markers • drawing paper • sea animal picture books

Children draw animals on **Blackline Masters 39–40**. They also draw sea creatures. Later in the week children draw and sort pictures of fruit. See pages T127, T137, and T145 for the activities.

fur/bear   feathers/duck

Art Center

Materials • drawing paper • water color or tempera paints

Children draw and label pictures of their favorite animal from *I Went Walking*. See page T133 for this week's Art Center activity.

1 yellow dog

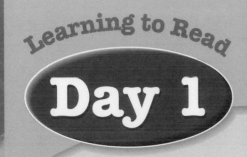

Day at a Glance

Learning to Read

Teacher Read Aloud:

How the Birds Got Their Colors

✓ Learning About / r /, page T120

Word Work

✓ **High-Frequency Word Practice,** page T122

Writing & Language

Oral Language, *page T123*

 Half-Day Kindergarten

✓ Indicates lessons for tested skills. Choose additional activities as time allows.

Opening

Calendar

Sunday	Monday	Tuesday	Wednesday	Thursday	Friday	Saturday
			1	2	3	4
5	6	7	8	9	10	11
12	13	14	15	16	17	18
19	20	21	22	23	24	25
26	27	28	29	30	31	

To begin the new week, ask a volunteer to find today's date on the calendar. Then review the days of the week. Together count the number of days left in the month.

Daily Message

Modeled Writing Incorporate the colors of children's clothing into the daily message.

> Sean has a canary yellow shirt. Kristen has a cardinal red dress. Today we'll read how the birds got their colors.

Ask children to find and read the word they added to the Word Wall last week. Then chant the spelling of the words on the wall with children: s-e-e *spells* see; *capital* I *spells* I, *capital* I *spells* I.

Daily Phonemic Awareness
Beginning Sounds

- *Listen:* rrring, rrrake. *Say the words with me:* ring, rake. *Do* ring *and* rake *begin with the same sound?... Yes,* ring *and* rake *begin with the same sound,* /r/.

- Play Same Sound Sort, reviewing the rules before you begin.

cap/cake	goat/pig
milk/mat	hat/coat
rain/room	sun/sand
book/bed	rice/rope
six/five	

Syllables in Spoken Words

- Tell children that today, they will clap the word parts in bird names.

- *Listen:* hum-ming-bird. *Say* hum-ming-bird. *How many claps did you hear?... That's right, three.*

- Continue the names of other birds, for example: cardinal, goldfinch, bluejay, woodpecker, owl, canary, robin, sandpiper, pelican.

Getting Ready to Learn

To help plan their day, tell children that they will

- listen to a story called *How the Birds Got Their Colors.*

- meet a new Alphafriend, Reggie Rooster.

- act out a story in the Dramatic Play Center.

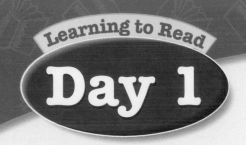

Day 1

Read Aloud

Purposes • oral language • listening strategy
• comprehension skill

Selection Summary

In this porquoi tale, Rascal Raccoon covers Wolf's eyes with mud while he is napping. When Wolf awakes, he can't see. Fortunately, the woodland birds peck the hardened mud from his eyes. To thank them, Wolf paints them different colors. He then forgives Raccoon and paints her a mischievous mask.

Key Concept
Colors of birds

English Language Learners

Before reading, share picture books on birds to familiarize children with the birds mentioned in the selection. You may want to point out birds common to your area.

Teacher Read Aloud
Oral Language/Comprehension

▶ **Building Background**

Have children describe some of the birds they have seen. Guide the discussion so they talk about brightly colored birds as well as those that have markings such as spots, stripes, and speckles.

As you display the illustration, tell children that today's story is a porquoi tale, a story that tells how something happened. Explain that this tale came from North and South America and tells how the birds got their colors.

Strategy: Predict/Infer

Teacher Modeling Remind children that good readers think about what a story will be about. They make predictions about what will happen, and then as they read they check to see if their predictions were correct. *Look at the illustration. What do you think this story is about? Do you see birds in the picture? What colors are they? What else is in the picture? As we read, we'll check our predictions.*

 ### Comprehension Focus: Sequence of Events

Teacher Modeling Remind children that good readers try to remember what happens at the beginning of a story, in the middle, and at the end. Doing this helps them remember the order of events. Often the beginning is where you find out the problem. Ask: *What is the problem in this story?*

▶ Listening to the Story

As you read the story aloud, pause at the discussion points so that children can sequence the events. Note that the Read Aloud art is also available on the back of the Theme poster.

▶ Responding

Summarizing the Story Help children summarize parts of the story.

- *What happened at the beginning of the story? Why did Raccoon put mud over Wolf's eyes?*

- *What happened when Wolf woke up? How did the birds help him?*

- *What did Wolf do after his eyes were clear again?*

- *What did Wolf do at the end of the story?*

- *What was your favorite part of the story?*

Practice Book pages 65–66 Children will complete the pages at small group time.

Practice Book p. 66

Name _____

Practice Book p. 65

Name _____

1   2   3

At Group Time

Dramatic Play Center

Materials • paper lunch bags • colored markers • colored paper

Prepare large paper-bag puppets for Wolf and Raccoon. Children make lunch-bag sized puppets for the birds. One side of the paper bag can show a gray bird; the other side a brightly colored or patterned bird. Children can use the puppets to act out the story and take turns playing the roles of Wolf and Raccoon.

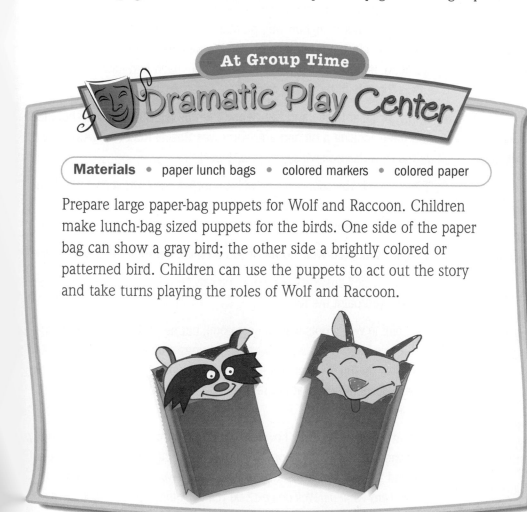

Teacher's Note

Metaphor On a rereading, point out descriptive phrases such as... *hear the wind dancing through the trees* and... *rushed to his side in a great cloud of feathers.*

How the Birds Got Their Colors

A Porquoi Tale Told in North and South America

How did the birds get their colors? Have you ever wondered about that? Some folks say the birds can thank the wolf for their beautiful colors.

Long ago, all the birds and animals in the forest shared and helped one another. One of the strongest and most helpful of them all was Wolf. He was the fastest runner and best hunter, and he always shared what he had. Raccoon shared too, but she was mischievous, so it was mostly pranks and tricks that she shared. She was such a trouble maker in fact, that everyone called her Rascal Raccoon.

One day Rascal Raccoon annoyed Wolf so much that he chased her up a tree. With Racoon up in the tree, Wolf decided to take a nap. When Wolf was sound asleep, Raccoon crept down the tree. "Now is my chance to play a great trick on Wolf," she thought.

So Raccoon set to work scooping mud from the soft, wet ground. She spread it over Wolf's eyes, where it dried, hard as clay. Then she hid nearby to see what would happen. (**Ask:** *What happened to Rascal Raccoon first on this day? What did she do next? After that?*)

Soon Wolf began to stretch and yawn. He could hear the wind dancing through the trees, and he could smell the scent of wildflowers. But when he tried to open his great green eyes, it was dark!

"O-w-o-o-o," howled Wolf. "I cannot see. What will become of me?" (**Ask:** *Why can't Wolf see? Do you think anyone will help him?*)

The birds were the first to hear Wolf's cries. They rushed to his side in a great cloud of feathers. It was hard to tell one bird from another because all the birds were the same color—dull gray. The birds looked closely at Wolf; soon they found out what was wrong. Rascal Raccoon was rolling with laughter as she watched. She had never seen anything so silly.

At last Wise Old Owl called for silence. "I have an idea," he said. "We can peck the mud from Wolf's eyes." The birds pecked carefully because they didn't want to hurt their friend. After many hours, Wolf's great green eyes finally opened wide again. "Thank you, thank you, my little feathered friends," he called. "How can I repay your kindness? I will do anything I can for you."

All the birds thought and thought, until, finally, a tiny gray hummingbird spoke up. "Please, Wolf," begged Hummingbird, "We don't like being dull and gray. The wildflowers and butterflies are such beautiful colors. We were wondering if you could make all of us bright colors too."

"That's a wonderful idea!" exclaimed Wolf. "I'll see what I can do." So he got some paint pots from his den. Then he set about making some brilliant colors. He used purple from berries, red from roses, yellow from marigolds, and green from leaves. Wolf mixed the colors and sprinkled little flecks of gold from the sun over all.

When Wolf was ready, Cardinal flew to the front of the line, asking to be the first to get his new color. Wolf painted him a bright red color. Next came a small finch. Wolf painted him gold and black. "From now on," said Wolf, "you will be known as Goldfinch!"

The jay was painted blue and white and black. Now he would be called Blue Jay. The hummingbird was painted bright green and the mallard's colors were shiny and dark. Wolf gave Woodpecker stripes, spots, and a red head, and Owl got speckles. One by one, each bird flew off to brighten the forest with their new colors.

At last, Wolf sat back, tired but happy. Then he felt a tap on his shoulder. And there, looking a bit sad and sorry, was Rascal Raccoon. (**Ask:** *What do you think Raccoon will say and do? Why?*)

"Please, Wolf," Raccoon asked, "will you forgive me? I'm sorry I played a trick on you. I saw how kind the birds were to you and the reward you gave them in return."

"I forgive you," said Wolf slowly, "if you promise not to tease anyone."

"Oh, I promise," answered Raccoon, quickly. "But I want to ask a favor of you. Will you paint me too?"

The paint in Wolf's pots was almost gone, but he had some lovely black and brown left. So he used that to paint rings around Raccoon's tail. And then—just for fun—he painted a black mask around Raccoon's eyes. When Raccoon looked at her reflection in the pond, she was very pleased.

So that's one story about how birds got the bright colors they wear today. And when you see a raccoon, you'll remember the story about how it got a ringed tail and black mask. (**Say:** *For awhile, Wolf couldn't see. Who helped him? What did Wolf do next? Do you think this is a story that could really happen?*)

Day 1

Children

- identify pictures whose names begin with /r/

MATERIALS

- **Alphafriend Cards** *Mimi Mouse, Reggie Rooster, Sammy Seal*
- **Alphafriend Audiotape** *Theme 2*
- **Alphafolder** *Reggie Rooster*
- **Picture Cards** *man, map, mop, rock, rope, rug, salt, sandals, sun*
- **Phonics Center:** *Theme 2, Week 3, Day 1*

Home Connection

A take-home version of Reggie Rooster's Song is on an **Alphafriends Blackline Master.** Children can share the song with their families.

English Language Learners

Because the English *r* is different from most *r* sounds in other languages, many children have difficulty pronouncing the /r/ sound. Display Picture Cards for *r*. Then name each picture with children.

Phonemic Awareness

☑ *Beginning Sound*

▶ Introducing the Alphafriend: Reggie Rooster

Tell children that today they will meet a new Alphafriend. Recall with children that Alphafriends are friends that help them to remember the sounds the letters of the alphabet make. Have children listen as you share a riddle to help them guess who their new Alphafriend is.

1 **Alphafriend Riddle** Read these clues:

- *Our Alphafriend's sound is /r/. Say it with me: /r/.*
- *This feathered animal has a rrred cap on his head.*
- *He rrrules the barnyard and the rrroost.*
- *He wakes up the whole farm with a "cock-a-doodle-doo."*

When most hands are up, call on children until they guess *rooster*.

2 **Pocket Chart** Display Reggie Rooster in a pocket chart. Say his name, stretching the /r/ sound slightly, and have children echo the sound.

3  **Alphafriend Audiotape** Play Reggie Rooster's song. Listen for /r/ words in Reggie's song.

4 **Alphafolder** Have children find the /r/ pictures in the scene.

5 **Summarize**

- *What is our Alphafriend's name? What is his sound?*
- *What words in our Alphafriend's song start with /r/?*
- *Each time you look at Reggie Rooster this week, remember the /r/ sound.*

Reggie Rooster's Song
(Tune: "Hush! Little Baby")

Reggie has a rocket that is red.
Reggie keeps it right beside his bed.
Reggie likes to listen to rock 'n roll.
Reggie plays it on his radio.

▶ Listening for / r /

Compare and Review: / m /, / s / Display Alphafriends *Mimi Mouse* and *Sammy Seal* opposite *Reggie Rooster.* Review each character's sound.

Tell children you'll name some pictures, and they should signal "thumbs up" for each one that starts with Reggie Rooster's sound, / r /. Volunteers put the card below Reggie's picture. For "thumbs down" words, volunteers put cards below the correct Alphafriends.

Pictures: *man, map, mop, rock, rope, rug, salt, sandals, sun*

Tell children they will sort more pictures in the Phonics Center today.

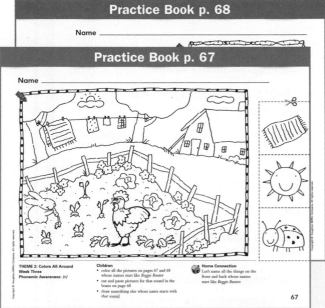

Practice Book p. 68

Name _____

Practice Book p. 67

Name _____

THEME 2: Colors All Around
Week Three
Phonemic Awareness: /r/

Children
• color all the pictures on pages 67 and 68 whose names start like *Reggie Rooster*
• cut and paste pictures for that sound in the boxes on page 68
• draw something else whose name starts with that sound

Home Connection
Let's name all the things on the front and back whose names start like *Reggie Rooster.*

67

▶ Apply

Practice Book pages 67–68 Children will complete the pages at small group time.

At Group Time

Phonics Center

Use the Phonics Center materials for **Theme 2, Week 3, Day 1**.

High-Frequency Word Practice

▶ Matching Words

■ Display the Word Cards for the high-frequency words *I* and *see* in a pocket chart. Have children read each word and match it on the Word Wall.

■ Remind children that these words are often found in books. *I'll read a poem. You listen to hear if these words are used in it.*

■ Read the poem "Tommy" on page 38 of *Higglety Pigglety. Did you hear the*

Tommy

I put a seed into the ground
And said, "I'll watch it grow."
I watered it and cared for it
As well as I could know.

One day I walked in my back yard,
And oh, what did I see!
My seed had popped itself right out,
Without consulting me.

by Gwendolyn Brooks

38

***Higglety Pigglety: A Book of Rhymes,* page 38**

words I *and* see *in the poem? Let's see if you can match the Word Cards* I *and* see *to the words* I *and* see *in the poem.*

Writing Opportunity Place the Word Cards *I see* in a pocket chart as a sentence stem. Then display the Picture Cards *berries, red, sandals,* and *toys*. Help children build sentences with the cards. Children may then write and illustrate one of the sentences or use the words to create their own sentences with rebus pictures.

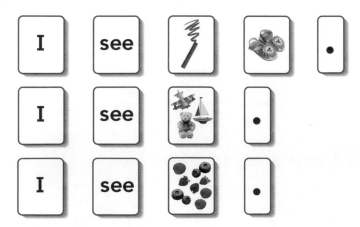

Oral Language

▶ Using Singular and Plural Words

Viewing and Speaking Remind children that some words are nouns, or naming words. These words name people, places, and things. Display *How the Birds Got Their Colors.* **Use naming words to tell me what you see in the picture.** Write children's responses on chart paper, listing singular nouns in one column and plural nouns in another.

■ *What do you notice about the words in the second column?* Explain that some naming words name one person or one thing, while others name more than one person or thing. *We add the letter* s *or sometimes* es *to a naming word to mean "more than one."*

One	More Than One
raccoon	birds
wolf	flowers
tree	trees

Portfolio Opportunity
Save children's work as examples of their ability to distinguish between singular and plural nouns.

At Group Time

Writing Center

Place the chart in the Writing Center. Tell children to draw a picture of one person, animal, or object on one half of the paper. On the other half, they will draw more than one person, animal, or object. Encourage children to label their pictures, using what they know about letters and their sounds. Remind children they can also refer to charts, labels, the Word Wall, and books as they write.

bird   birds

English Language Learners

Most children will not have problems adding "s" to form plural nouns, but they may be confused that the article stays the same. Help children to name and label their pictures accordingly, for example: *the bird; the birds.*

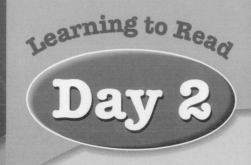

Learning to Read
Day 2

Day at a Glance

Learning to Read

Big Book:

I Went Walking

☑ **Phonics:**
Initial
Consonant *r,*
page T128

☑ **High-**
Frequency
Words: *I, see, page T130*

Word Work

High-Frequency Word Practice,
page T132

Writing & Language

Vocabulary Expansion, *page T133*

 Half-Day Kindergarten

☑ Indicates lessons for tested
skills. Choose additional
activities as time allows.

Opening

Calendar

Sunday	Monday	Tuesday	Wednesday	Thursday	Friday	Saturday
			1	2	3	4
5	6	7	8	9	10	11
12	13	14	15	16	17	18
19	20	21	22	23	24	25
26	27	28	29	30	31	

Find today's date on the
calendar with the children.
Count how many more
school days there are in the
week. Talk about special
events that will occur soon.

Daily Message

Modeled Writing As you write the
daily message, model for children
what you are doing: *The first word in
a sentence begins with a capital letter. The first word in my sentence is
today, so I will begin writing with a
capital* T.

Today we will
go outside
at 10:30.

Have children find and read the words they've added to the Word Wall.
Chant the spellings with children. Then have volunteers use the words in
oral sentences.

Daily Phonemic Awareness
Beginning Sounds

- *Let's listen for beginning sounds. I'll say two words, you tell me which word begins with Reggie Rooster's sound, /r/. Listen: red, yellow. Say the words with me:* red, yellow. *Which word begins with /r/?... Yes,* red *begins with /r/.*

- Continue with other words.

Syllables in Spoken Words

- Read aloud "Everybody Says" on page 6 of *Higglety Pigglety.*

- Tell children they'll clap the word parts they hear in words from the poem.

- *Listen:* mother, moth-er. *Say* mother *again, clapping the syllables. How many claps did you hear?... Yes, two! Now say and clap the word with me:* moth-er.

- Continue with other words from the poem.

bed/rice
mat/rug
silly/rain
boy/rose
path/ring
ribbon/big
sing/rock
walk/riddle
ring/now

Getting Ready to Learn

To help plan their day, tell children that they will

- listen to a Big Book: *I Went Walking.*

- learn the new letters *R* and *r,* and see words that begin with *r.*

- explore animals in the Science Center.

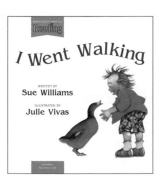

Day 2

Big Book

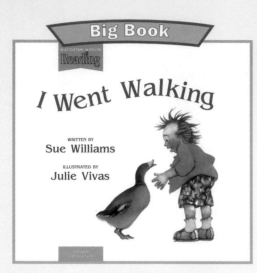

I Went Walking

WRITTEN BY
Sue Williams

ILLUSTRATED BY
Julie Vivas

Purposes • concepts of print • story language
• reading strategy • comprehension skill

English Language Learners

As you reread, ask children to predict which animal the boy will see next. After reading, have children retell the story as closely as they can remember. Write their sentences on chart paper or have them draw pictures. Children can check the book to compare the sequences of events.

Sharing the Big Book
Oral Language/Comprehension

▶ Building Background

Reading for Understanding *You remember this book,* I Went Walking. *This time when we read the book, think about whether the animals have fur, feathers, skin, or scales.*

Strategy: Predict/Infer

Student Modeling Review that good readers make predictions about a book, and then check their predictions as they read. *What can you predict about the story from the title and the cover picture?*

Comprehension Focus:
Inferences: Making Predictions

Student Modeling *Who is telling the story? Can I tell from the cover where the story takes place?*

▶ Sharing the Story

Reread the story, pausing for these discussion points:

 pages 8–9
Comprehension: Sequence of Events

■ *What was the first animal the boy saw? What animal did the boy see next?*

 page 11
Concepts of Print: Capital at Beginning of a Sentence; End Punctuation

■ *What is different about the first letter of the sentence? What do you know about the mark at the end of the sentence?*

pages 16–17

Compare and Contrast

■ *How is the duck different from the other animals the boy has seen?*

 pages 18–19

Comprehension: Sequence of Events

■ *What animals have we met so far? What colors are these animals? What animal will we meet next?*

▶ **Responding**

Reader's Theater Have partners act out the story. One child asks, *What did you see?* while the other child answers. If necessary, use the book to prompt children's answers.

At Group Time

Science Center

> **Materials** • Blackline Masters 39–40 • nonfiction animal picture books • crayons

Prepare copies of **Blackline Masters 39–40.** Children can draw pictures to show animals with fur, feathers, scales, or skin. They may wish to refer to the picture books as they brainstorm animals to fit the different categories.

fur/bear   feathers/duck

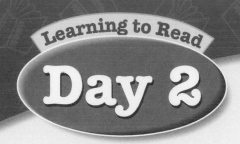

Phonics

✓ *Initial Consonant r*

▶ Develop Phonemic Awareness

Beginning Sound Read the lyrics to Reggie Rooster's song and have children echo it line-for-line. Have them listen for the /r/ words and "rub" their stomachs each time they hear one.

> **Reggie Rooster's Song**
> (Tune: "Hush! Little Baby")
>
> Reggie has a rocket that is red.
> Reggie keeps it right beside
>   his bed.
> Reggie likes to listen to
>   rock 'n roll.
> Reggie plays it on his radio.

▶ Connect Sounds to Letters

Beginning Letter Display the *Reggie Rooster* card, and have children name the letter on the picture. Say: *The letter* r *stands for the sound /r/, as in* rooster. *When you see an* r, *remember* Reggie Rooster. *That will help you remember the sound /r/.*

Write *rooster* on the board, underlining the *r*. *What is the first letter in the word* rooster? *(r)* Rooster *starts with /r/, so* r *is the first letter I write for* rooster.

Compare and Review: *m, s* In a pocket chart, display the Letter Cards *r, m,* and *s*. Place the Picture Cards in random order. Review the sounds for *r, m,* and *s*. Taking turns, children can name a picture, say the beginning sound, and put the card below the correct letter.

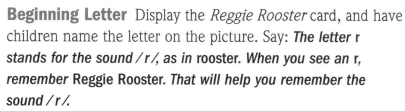

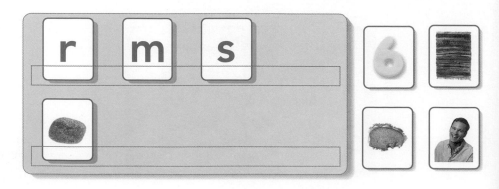

Tell children they will sort more pictures in the Phonics Center today.

▶ Handwriting

Writing R, r Tell children that now they'll learn to write the letters that stand for /r/: capital *R* and small *r*. Write each letter as you recite the handwriting rhyme. Children can chant each rhyme as they "write" the letter in the air.

Handwriting Rhyme: R

Make a line down, straight and tall. Curve around to the middle. A short line out, that's all!

Handwriting Rhyme: r

Little *r* is small. Start in the middle with a short line. Curve at the top, that's all!

▶ Apply

Practice Book page 69 Children will complete this page at small group time.

Blackline Master 174 This page provides additional handwriting practice.

Phonics Center

Use Phonics Center materials for **Theme 2, Week 3, Day 2**.

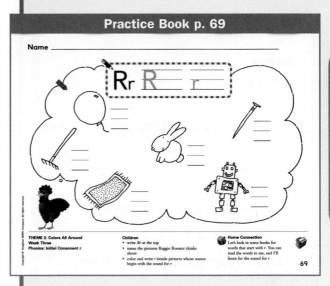

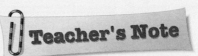

📎 Teacher's Note

Handwriting practice for the continuous stroke style is available on **Blackline Master 200**.

Portfolio Opportunity

Save the Practice Book page to show children's grasp of the letter-sound association.
Save **Blackline Master 174** for a handwriting sample.

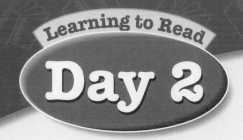
☑ High-Frequency Words
Review Words: I, see

▶ Teach

Tell children that today they will practice reading and writing two words that they will see often in stories. Say *I* and call on volunteers to use the word in context.

Write *I* on the board, and have children spell it as you point to the letters. **Spell I with me, capital I, I.** Then lead children in a chant, clapping on each beat, to help them remember the spelling: **capital I, I!** **capital I, I.** Repeat for the word *see*.

 Have children find the words *I* and *see* on the Word Wall. Remind children to look there when they need to remember how to write the words.

▶ Practice

Reading Display the following sentences in a pocket chart. Children take turns reading the sentences aloud. Leave out the pocket chart along with additional Picture Cards so that children can practice making and reading sentences.

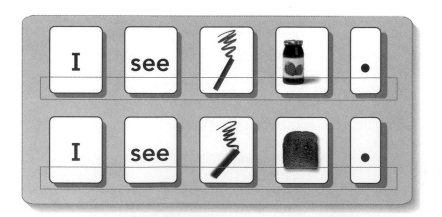

Display *Higglety Pigglety: A Book of Rhymes*, page 44.

■ Share the poem "Rhyme" aloud.

■ *I'll read the poem one more time. This time, listen for the word I. If you hear it raise your hand.*

■ Call on children to point to the word *I* each time it appears in the poem.

■ Repeat for the word *see.*

Higglety Pigglety: A Book of Rhymes, page 44

Diagnostic Check

If . . .	You can . . .
children have problems reading *I* or *see* in the poem,	have them build the words with magnetic letters and use them in oral sentences.

Word Work

Day 2

OBJECTIVES

Children
- read high-frequency words
- create and write sentences with high-frequency words

MATERIALS

- **Word Cards** *I, see*
- **Picture Cards** *berries, blue, red;* choose others for sentence building
- **Punctuation Card:** period

High-Frequency Word Practice

▶ Building Sentences

Tell children that you want to build a sentence and need their help.

- Display the Word Cards and Picture Cards in random order. Tell children that you will use these words to make your sentence. Review the words together. Then explain that you are ready to begin.

- *I want the first word to be* **I.** *Who can find that word?*

- Continue until you have the stem *I see* _____.

- *The color I want is* **blue.** *Which card should I choose?* Have a volunteer place the *blue* card in the pocket chart.

- Place the Picture Card *berries* at the end of the sentence. Then read the completed sentence together.

- Continue with other sentences.

Writing Opportunity On paper or white boards have children copy the sentence stem *I see.* Then have children complete the sentence by drawing a picture of something that is a color they select. Some children may want to refer to the Color Chart to write color words.

Vocabulary Expansion

▶ ## Using Plural Names

Viewing and Speaking Display *I Went Walking*. Page through the book, asking children to name the animals they see. List their responses on chart paper.

■ Remind children that some nouns name one person, place, or thing and others name more than one. Read through the list with children, pointing out that each word names one: *cat, horse, cow, duck, pig,* and *dog.*

■ Read through the list a second time. Prompt children to provide the plural for each animal name. ***The word* cat *names one cat. What word names more than one cat?*** Write *cats,* explaining how you form the plural. ***I will add* s *to* cat *to name more than one cat,* cats.**

OBJECTIVES

Children
• name singular and plural animal names

MATERIALS

• **Big Book:** *I Went Walking*

DAY 2

One	More Than One
cat	cats
horse	horses
cow	cows
duck	ducks
pig	pigs
dog	dogs

At Group Time
Art Center

Materials • drawing paper • crayons or markers

Place the chart in the Art Center. Have children draw their favorite animal from *I Went Walking*. Children can refer to the chart to label their pictures.

1 yellow dog

English Language Learners

Display pictures that show several images of the same animal. Say the singular word as you point to one animal; say the plural word as you point to the animals collectively. Have children repeat after you. Listen for correct pronunciation of the plural endings, especially the voiced ending on *pigs* and *dogs.*

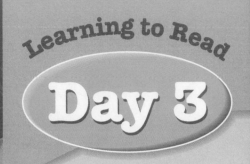

Day at a Glance

Learning to Read

Big Book:

In the Big Blue Sea

 Phonics: Initial Consonant *r*, page T138

Word Work

Exploring Words, *page T140*

Writing & Language

Shared Writing, *page T141*

 Half-Day Kindergarten

 Indicates lessons for tested skills. Choose additional activities as time allows.

Opening

Calendar

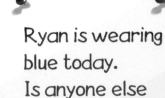

Sunday	Monday	Tuesday	Wednesday	Thursday	Friday	Saturday
			1	2	3	4
5	6	7	8	9	10	11
12	13	14	15	16	17	18
19	20	21	22	23	24	25
26	27	28	29	30	31	

Review the days of the week. Count the number of Wednesdays in the month compared to the number of Tuesdays and Thursdays. Write today's date on the board.

Daily Message

Modeled Writing Promote a color when you write the daily message. *Today when you help me write, you'll use a (blue) marker. Then we'll see how much you were able to help me.* Call on children to write their names or the initial consonants of known letters.

> Ryan is wearing blue today.
> Is anyone else wearing blue?

Have children find *I* and *see,* the words they added to the Word Wall this theme. Then ask them to chant the spellings of the words with you. Call on volunteers to use the words in oral sentences.

Routines

 ## Daily Phonemic Awareness
Beginning Sounds

- Display, in random order, Picture Cards for: *map, man, hug, hose, rake, rope, web, wig.*

- Play a beginning sound game. Hold up Picture Card *rope.* **Say rrrope with me. Now listen as I name the other pictures. Raise your hand when you hear a word that begins with the same sound as rrrope.**

- When most hands are up, have children name the picture that begins like *rope.* (*rake*) Continue until all the Picture Cards have been matched by beginning sound.

✓ Syllables in Spoken Words

- *Listen: roost-er. Clap with me: Rooster. How many claps did you hear?... Yes, two!*

- Continue with other animal names: *chicken, duckling, piglet, monkey, elephant, octopus, camel, panda, hippopotamus.*

Getting Ready to Learn

To help plan their day, tell children that they will

- reread and talk about the Big Book: *In the Big Blue Sea.*

- read a story called "The Parade."

- explore sea animals in the Science Center.

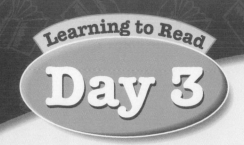

Day 3

Big Book

Reading

In the Big Blue Sea

by Chyng Feng Sun
Photography by Norbert Wu

Includes:
Science Link

Purposes • concepts of print • story language
• reading strategy • comprehension skill

Sharing the Big Book
Oral Language/Comprehension

▶ **Building Background**

Reading for Understanding Display the book and read the title aloud. Remind children that the pictures in this book were taken by Norbert Wu. Tell children that this time when we read the story, they can think of other color words that will describe the fish.

> **title page**
>
> ## Strategy: Summarize
>
> **Student Modeling** Remind children that good readers think about the important information in a story so that they can talk about it later.
>
> ■ *What do you remember about this story? What kind of information will you look for as we read the story today?*
>
> **title page**
>
> ## Comprehension Focus:
> ## Inferences: Making Predictions
>
> ■ *Let's read the title and look at the picture. What do these tell you about the book?*

Extra Support

Review the story pictures with children, having them name the color of the fish on each page.

▶ Sharing the Story

Reread the story, pausing for these discussion points:

page 1
Noting Details

■ *Where does Norbert Wu take his pictures?*

pages 4–7
Summarize

■ *What color fish have we read about so far? Were the fish all one color or did they have different colors? Tell more about the fish.*

pages 16–17
Compare and Contrast

■ *How were the children and Norbert Wu like fish? How were they different?*

▶ Responding

Children take turns sharing information about the fish using picture clues as prompts. Page through the book more than once so all children have a chance to participate.

Practice Book page 70 Children complete the page at small group time.

Science Center

Materials • nonfiction picture books about the sea • drawing paper • crayons

Place nonfiction picture books about the sea in the Science Center. Have children browse through the books. Then ask them to draw pictures of other animals that live in the sea.

DAY 3

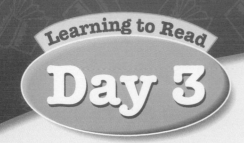

OBJECTIVES

Children

- identify words that begin with / r /
- identify pictures whose names start with the letter *r*

MATERIALS

- **Alphafriend Card** *Reggie Rooster*
- **Alphafriend Audiotape** Theme 2
- **Picture Cards** for *r* and assorted others

Extra Support

Read "Rainy Day," *Higglety Pigglety: A Book of Rhymes* page 13. Have children touch a finger to their mouth each time they hear a word that begins with / r /. Then call on volunteers to point to words that begin with *r* in the rhyme.

Phonics

✓ Initial Consonant r

▶ Develop Phonemic Awareness

Beginning Sound Read the lyrics to Reggie Rooster's song aloud, and have children clap for each / r / word.

Tell children that you will read the song again. *This time, if you hear a word that begins with / r / stand up. If you hear another / r / word, sit down. We'll do this each time we hear a / r / word.* As needed, model standing and sitting alternately for / r / words as you read the first line. Then reread the poem, having children stand and sit for / r / words.

> **Reggie Rooster's Song**
> (Tune: "Hush! Little Baby")
>
> Reggie has a rocket that is red.
> Reggie keeps it right beside
>   his bed.
> Reggie likes to listen to
>   rock 'n roll.
> Reggie plays it on his radio.

▶ Connect Sounds to Letters

Beginning Letter r Display the Reggie Rooster card and have children name the letter on the picture. *What letter stands for the sound / r /, as in rooster?* (r) *Who can help you remember the sound / r /?* (Reggie Rooster)

Write *rooster* on the board, underlining *r*. **What is the first letter in rooster?** (r) *Rooster* starts with / r /, so *r* is the first letter I write for *rooster*.

Compare and Review Write *Rr* on the board and circle it. Then write *Rr*, circle it, and draw a line through it to represent "not *r*." Distribute Picture Cards for *r* and assorted other Picture Cards, one to a child, to a group of children. In turn, children name the picture, say the beginning sound, and stand below the correct symbol on the board.

Repeat the activity with different groups of children until each child has a chance to name a picture, say the beginning sound, and stand below the correct symbol on the board.

Phonics in Action

Applying Skills

▶ Introducing the Story

Let's read the title. The title is "The Parade." I see animals on this page. What are all of the animals holding? What kind of a parade do you think this is? Let's look at the pictures to see what the story is about. As you do a picture walk, guide children in a discussion of the pictures.

▶ Coached Reading

Have children look carefully at each page before discussing it with you. Prompts:

page 18   *What animal do you see? What is the pig doing?* (a pig; The pig is inviting others to join in the parade.)

page 19   *Did anyone join in the parade? Who?*

page 20   *What instrument is the cow playing?*

page 20   *What is the frog doing?*

pages 22–23   *Who else joined the parade? Why are all of the animals running away?*

Now let's go back and look at each page to find things that begin with Reggie Rooster's sound, /r/.

Phonics Library

Purposes
- read a wordless story
- find pictures beginning with /r/

The Parade
by Susan Gorman-Howe
illustrated by Joan Paley

17

18   19

20   21

22   23

DAY 3

Home Connection

Children can color the pictures in the take-home version of "The Parade." After rereading on Day 4, children can take it home to read to family members.

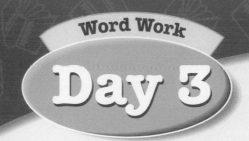
Exploring Words

 ## Color Words

Have children recall the colors of fish in *In the Big Blue Sea.* Then display the book. Explain to children that often animals are not all one color. Like the birds in *How the Birds Got Their Colors,* animals can have patterns, spots, stripes, and flecks of different colors in them.

- Open the book to pages 4 and 5. Read aloud the text, and write the word *green* on chart paper. Then point to page 4. **Is this fish only *green* or mostly *green*? What other colors do you see? How would you describe this fish?**

- Repeat with the other fish featured in the story.

Writing Opportunity Have children think about the different colors animals can be. Then ask children to draw a picture of any animal they wish. Tell children to label their drawings by writing the color words that describe the animal. Children can refer to the color words listed on *From Apples to Zebras,* page 29.

Shared Writing

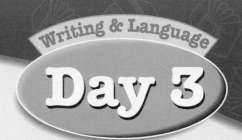

▶ Writing a Graphic Organizer

Display the list you began in the Word Work activity on page T140. Read the words with children, reminding them that these were the colors of the fish in *In the Big Blue Sea*. Write *In the Big Blue Sea* as a column heading. Then page through the book. For each color on the chart, write the word *fish* under the heading.

■ Recall with children that they have read about many different animals and their colors. Use the chart as a basis for creating a graphic organizer for the animals and colors children have read about.

■ Create a column for *I Went Walking*. Point to the word *green* on the list. **Was there a green animal in this book? Who can find it for me? Yes, the duck was green.** Write *duck* on the chart.

■ Proceed in a similar manner, having children raise their hands when they hear the color of an animal as you reread *How the Birds Got Their Colors*.

OBJECTIVES

Children
- write a graphic organizer

MATERIALS

- **Big Book:** *In the Big Blue Sea*
- **Big Book:** *I Went Walking*
- **Teacher Read Aloud:** *How the Birds Got Their Colors*

DAY 3

	In the Big Blue Sea	I Went Walking	How the Birds Got Their Colors
green	fish	duck	hummingbird
red	fish	cow	cardinal
yellow	fish	dog	goldfinch
orange	fish		
white	fish		
blue	fish		bluejay
purple	fish		
black	fish	cat	raccoon
brown		horse	

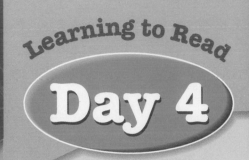

Day 4

Day at a Glance

Learning to Read

Big Books:

What's My Favorite Color?

What Do You Do, Norbert Wu?

 Phonics: Review Initial Consonant *r*, page T146

Word Work

Exploring Words, *page T148*

Writing & Language

Interactive Writing, *page T149*

 Half-Day Kindergarten

☑ Indicates lessons for tested skills. Choose additional activities as time allows.

Opening

Calendar

Sunday	Monday	Tuesday	Wednesday	Thursday	Friday	Saturday
			1	2	3	4
5	6	7	8	9	10	11
12	13	14	15	16	17	18
19	20	21	22	23	24	25
26	27	28	29	30	31	

Find today's date on the calendar. Review the month and the day of the week. Then ask children to tell the name of the season, and talk about today's weather.

Daily Message

Modeled Writing Use some words that begin with *r* in today's message, as in the example shown.

> Today, we will change the rabbit's cage. Reba and Tina will help.

Ask children to find and read the words that they've added to the Word Wall. Call on volunteers to point to the words and read them. Have children chant the spellings: *capital* **I** *spells* **I**; s-e-e *spells* see.

Routines

✓ Daily Phonemic Awareness
Beginning Sounds

- *Listen: radio, ring. Say the words with me: radio, ring. Do you hear the same sound at the beginning of each word?... Yes, radio and ring begin with the same sound.* Help children isolate the beginning sound, /r/.

- Play a listening game with children. *I will say two words. You listen carefully to tell me what the beginning sound is.*

road/river   sip/sing

song/sink   silly/silver

middle/man   miss/meat

mud/money   red/ride

rip/ring

✓ Syllables in Spoken Words

- Remind children that they've been clapping the number of word parts they hear in words. **Today, we'll take turns listening for word parts in our names.**

- Demonstrate using your own name, for example *Baxter*. **Listen: Bax-ter. How many sounds did you hear? Clap the name with me.** Say *Bax-ter* again, clapping the syllables. Have children take turns using their own names.

Getting Ready to Learn

To help plan their day, tell children that they will

- reread the Science Links: *What's My Favorite Color?* and *What Do You Do, Norbert Wu?*

- sort words that begin with /n/ in the Phonics Center.

- reread a book called "The Parade."

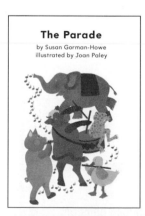

The Parade
by Susan Gorman-Howe
illustrated by Joan Paley

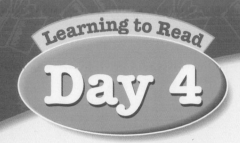

Big Book

pages 33–38

 Extra Support

Before rereading the Links, choose pairs of children to revisit the selections by taking picture walks through them. Children can take turns sharing what they remember about the selections using the pictures as prompts.

Sharing the Big Books
Science Link

▶ **Building Background**

Reading for Understanding As we read *What's My Favorite Color?*, think about other fruits that are the same colors. Pause for discussion as you share the story.

page 33

Strategy: Predict/Infer

Student Modeling Point out to children that the title asks a question. *What fruits do you see? What colors are they?*

 pages 34–35
Comprehension Focus: Inferences: Making Predictions

Student Modeling *What do you think the next page will show?* (a green fruit; pears) *Why do you think that?*

 page 36
Comprehension Focus: Sequence of Events

Student Modeling *What does the author say first, next, and last? How does what the author says help you predict what fruit will be shown next?*

 page 36
Concepts of Print: Capital at Beginning of Sentence, End Punctuation

■ *How many sentences are on this page? What can you tell me about the way each sentence begins and ends?*

▶ **Responding**

Personal Response Have children respond to the question *What color is you. favorite fruit?*

Science Link

▶ Building Background

Reading for Understanding As you read *What Do You Do, Norbert Wu?*, have children think about underwater photographs they might like to take. Pause for discussion as you reread the selection.

title page
Strategy: Summarize
Student Modeling *When you tell about this selection, what question should you answer?* (the title question)

✓ **page 21**
Comprehension Focus: Inferences: Making Predictions
Student Modeling *How does the cover help you predict what Norbert Wu does?*

✓ **page 26**
Concepts of Print: Capital at Beginning of Sentence, End Punctuation

■ *What can you tell me about the way this sentence begins and ends?*

▶ Responding

Literature Circle Have children tell how *What's My Favorite Color?* and *What Do You Do, Norbert Wu?* are alike. Then have them tell how they are different.

Science Center

(**Materials** • drawing paper • crayons or markers)

Have children draw pictures of different kinds of fruits they have eaten. Have small groups sort the pictures by color.

OBJECTIVES

Children
• make predictions
• recognize use of capital letter at the beginning of a sentence
• recognize use of end punctuation: period, question mark

Big Book

What Do You Do, Norbert Wu?

In the Big Blue Sea
by Chyng Feng Sun
Photography by Norbert Wu

pages 21–26

DAY 4

MEETING INDIVIDUAL NEEDS Challenge

Children can cut out magazine pictures, paste them to pieces of paper, and complete the sentence stem: *I see a _____!* Click! to create pages for their own picture books using the language pattern from *What Do You Do, Norbert Wu?*

OBJECTIVES

Children

- identify words that begin with /r/
- identify pictures whose names start with the letter *r*

MATERIALS

- **Alphafriend Cards** *Mimi Mouse, Reggie Rooster, Sammy Seal*
- **Alphafolder** *Reggie Rooster*
- **Letter Cards** *r, m, s*
- **Picture Cards** *man, map, mix, mule, rock, rug, run, sad, seal, six, sun*
- ***From Apples to Zebras: A Book of ABC's,*** page 19
- **Phonics Center:** Theme 2, Week 3, Day 4

Home Connection

Challenge children to look at home for items or for names that begin with the consonant *r*. Children can draw pictures to show what they have found.

Phonics

 Review Initial Consonant r

▶ Develop Phonemic Awareness

Beginning Sound Display the scene in Reggie Rooster's Folder. *One thing I see in Reggie's room is a radio. Say* radio *with me. Does* radio *begin with the same sound as Reggie Rooster, /r/?* Call on volunteers to point to and name other items in the picture that begin with /r/.

▶ Connect Sounds to Letters

Review Consonant *r* Using self-stick notes, cover the words on page 19 of *From Apples to Zebras: A Book of ABC's.* Then display the page. Ask children what letter they expect to see first in each word and why. Uncover the words so that children can check their predictions.

Provide each child with a self-stick note and ask the child to write the letter *r* on it. Then have children take turns placing the self-stick notes on classroom objects whose names begin with /r/. Gather as a group, and list the children's suggestions on the board.

From Apples to Zebras: A Book of ABC's, page 19

▶ Apply

Compare and Review: *r, m, s* In a pocket chart, display the Alphafriend cards and the Letter Cards *r, m,* and *s.* Review the sounds for /m/ and /s/.

Hold up Picture Cards one at a time. Have children name a picture, say the beginning sound, and place the card below the correct letter.

Pictures: *seal, rock, map, rug, six, mule, run, sad, mix, sun, man*

Tell children they will sort more pictures in the Phonics Center today.

Practice Book page 71 Children will complete this page at small group time.

Phonics Library In groups today, children will also identify pictures that begin with initial *r* as they reread the **Phonics Library** story "The Parade." See suggestions, page 139.

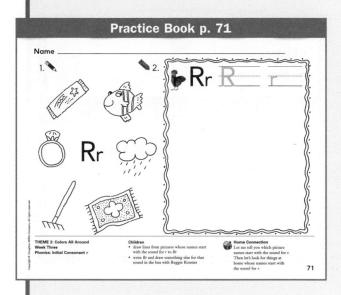

Phonics Center

Use Phonics Center materials for **Theme 2, Week 3, Day 4.**

Diagnostic Check

If ...	You can ...
children have trouble identifying /r/ words,	have them work with you or a partner to name items in the Alphafolder scene.

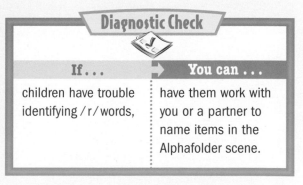

Phonics (T147)

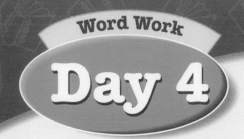
OBJECTIVES ◎

Children

• explore color words

MATERIALS

• *Higglety Pigglety: A Book of Rhymes,* page 10

• **Picture Cards:** blue, black, green, purple, orange, red color words

• **Blackline Master 41**

Exploring Words

▶ **Color Words**

Read aloud "I Love Colors" on page 10 of *Higglety Pigglety.*

■ Distribute Picture Cards to children. Have children match the cards to the words of the poem.

■ Tell children that you will reread the poem, this time you want them to hold their cards up in the air when they hear the color on their Picture Cards. Reread the poem slowly, pausing for children to respond when they hear the color word.

■ Repeat with other groups of children.

Higglety Pigglety: A Book of Rhymes, **page 10**

Writing Opportunity Place copies of **Blackline Master 41** in the Writing Center. Ask children to draw a picture using the colors mentioned in the poem. Help them to label their drawings.

Interactive Writing

▶ Writing a Class Story

Display the graphic organizer from yesterday's shared writing. Read through the chart with children.

- Point out that several of the stories you read included different animals that are the same colors, for example, a red fish, a red cow, and a red bird.

- Tell children that they are going to help you write a class story about the different colors and animals that they read about.

- Invite children to share the pen as you write the story. You may want to write the color words in the appropriate color.

> We read about a red fish, a red cow, and a red bird.
>
> The red bird is called a Cardinal.
>
> We also read about a yellow fish, a yellow dog, and a yellow bird.
>
> The yellow bird is called a Goldfinch.

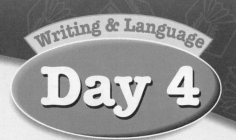
DAY 4

Day 5

Day at a Glance

Learning to Read

Revisiting the Literature:

How the Birds Got Their Colors, I Went Walking, In the Big Blue Sea, What's My Favorite Color? What Do You Do, Norbert Wu?, "The Parade"

✓ **Phonics: Initial Consonant *r*,** page T154

✓ **High-Frequency Word Review: *I, see*,** page T155

Word Work

Exploring Words, *page T156*

Writing & Language

Independent Writing, *page T157*

  Half-Day Kindergarten

✓ Indicates lessons for tested skills. Choose additional activities as time allows.

Opening

Calendar

Sunday	Monday	Tuesday	Wednesday	Thursday	Friday	Saturday
			1	2	3	4
5	6	7	8	9	10	11
12	13	14	15	16	17	18
19	20	21	22	23	24	25
26	27	28	29	30	31	

Have children review any words that were added to the calendar this week. Count how many days until upcoming special events.

Daily Message

Modeled Writing Have children help you write the daily message. *What kind of letter should I use to begin my sentence? How should I end the sentence, with a period or a question mark?*

Today is Annie's birthday. Shall we sing to her?

Read the Word Wall together, and then play a rhyming game: *Find a word on the wall that rhymes with my... Yes, I rhymes with my. Find a word on the wall that rhymes with tree... Yes, see rhymes with tree.*

Routines

☑ Daily Phonemic Awareness
Beginning Sounds

- Play a beginning sound game. Choose a child's name. Say: *I am thinking of someone's name. The name starts with /r/. Who has a name that starts with /r/?*

- Allow children to name all the possibilities before revealing the name you had in mind. Repeat with other names.

☑ Syllables in Spoken Words

- Remind children that they have been clapping the sounds they hear in words. *Now I'll say a word slowly. You put the parts together to guess the word I'm saying.*

- Choose the names of common classroom items. *Listen: cal-en-dar.* Have children say and clap the word parts: cal-en-dar. *How many claps did you hear?... Yes, three!*

- Continue with more words. (*teacher, boy, playground, goldfish, puzzle, window*)

Getting Ready to Learn

To help plan their day, tell children that they will

- reread and talk about all the books they've read this week.

- take home a story they can read.

- write in their journals.

The Parade
by Susan Gorman-Howe
illustrated by Joan Paley

I See.

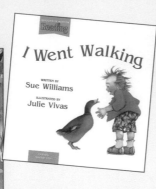

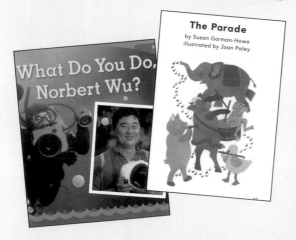

Revisiting the Literature

▶ **Literature Discussion**

Help children compare the different stories you have shared this week: *How the Birds Got Their Colors*, *I Went Walking*, *In the Big Blue Sea*, *What's My Favorite Color?*, *What Do You Do, Norbert Wu?* and "The Parade." Display the books one at a time. Use these suggestions to help children recall the selections.

■ Call on volunteers to tell what happened in *How the Birds Got Their Colors*.

■ Have children name the animals the boy saw in *I Went Walking*.

■ Ask children to tell what animals are featured in In the Big Blue Sea. **What colors of fish did we read about?**

■ Take a picture walk of *What Do You Do, Norbert Wu?* Ask if children remember what people with jobs like Norbert Wu's are called.

■ For *What's My Favorite Color?* call on volunteers to name the fruits mentioned by color.

■ Together, read "The Parade." Ask children to identify pictures beginning with /r/.

■ Children might also recall the Read Aloud stories I *Need a Lunch Box* and *Caps of Many Colors.* Have volunteers tell what they remember about these stories.

■ Have children vote for their favorite book, then read the text of the winner aloud.

✓ **Comprehension Focus: Making Predictions**

Display the books, one at a time, and read the titles aloud. Have children briefly tell what each story was about. Lead children in a discussion to tell how they used story and picture clues to make predictions about the stories and selections

✓ **Comprehension Focus: Sequence of Events**

Review the selections one at a time. Have children tell what happened first, next, and last in each story and identify the patterned order of events in each selection. After looking at each selection, help children develop a one- or two-sentence summary of it.

Technology
www.eduplace.com
Log on to **Education Place** for more activities relating to Colors All Around.

www.bookadventure.org
This Internet reading-incentive program provides thousands of titles for children to read.

Beautiful Butterflies

On My Way Practice Reader

▶ Preparing to Read

Building Background Read the title. Explain that this is an information book about real butterflies. Ask children to tell about the butterflies they have seen; explain that in this book they'll learn more about butterflies and their colors.

▶ Guiding the Narration

Together, look through the photographs and discuss them. Use the ideas below to prepare children for narrating the selection on their own.

page 1: *What colors do you see in the rainbow? What colors are the butterflies?*

pages 2-3: *Do you notice anything different about one of the butterflies? Most of these have the same colors, but butterflies come in other colors too. Where are the butterflies on page 3?.*

pages 4-5: *This is how a butterfly looks under a microscope, which makes things look bigger. What do you see? Where could a butterfly get water to drink?*

pages 6-7: *These are Monarch butterflies. What colors are they? Where could they go when it rains? When Monarchs travel in a big group, sometimes they all stop to rest. Monarchs often lay eggs on milkweed plants.*

page 8: *This is a butterfly ranch, where people go to see lots of butterflies. Would you like to visit a place like this? What would you try to find out about butterflies?*

Prompting the Narrators Have children take turns narrating the selection, page by page. Use prompts such as these:

- *What is the title of this book? What is it about?*

- *What colors are the butterflies? What can we learn from this page?*

Responding

Phonics Connection Have children look at the pictures for items whose names start with /s/, /m/, or /r/. Then children can draw pictures to show something they learned from the book and begin their own butterfly guide.

Leveled Books

The materials listed below provide reading practice for children at different levels.

Little Big Books

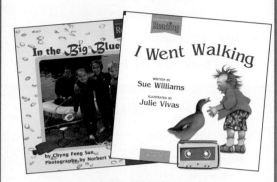

Little Readers for Guided Reading

Houghton Mifflin Classroom Bookshelf

DAY 5

 Home Connection

Remind children to share the take-home version of "The Parade" with their families.

Revisiting the Literature/
Building Fluency **(T153)**

Phonics Review

✓ Initial Consonants: r, m, s

▶ Review

Tell children that they will take turns naming pictures and telling what letter stands for the beginning sound.

- Randomly place four Picture Cards along the chalkboard ledge. Write *m, s,* and *r* on the board. Call on four children to come up and stand in front of a picture. In turn, have each child name the picture, isolate the initial sound, and point to *r, m,* or *s.*

- Have the rest of the class verify that the correct letter has been chosen. Then write the picture name on the board and underline the initial consonant.

- Continue until everyone has a chance to name a picture and point to the consonant that stands for its beginning sound.

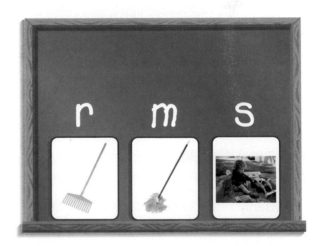

High-Frequency Word Review

✓ *I, see*

▶ Review

Give each small group the Word Cards, Picture Cards, and Punctuation Card needed to make a sentence. Each child holds one card. Children stand and arrange themselves to make a sentence for others to read.

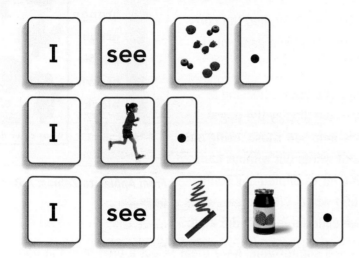

▶ Apply

Practice Book page 72 Children can complete this page independently and read it to you during small group time.

Phonics Library Have children take turns reading aloud to the class. Each child can discuss one page of "The Parade" or a favorite **Phonics Library** selection from the previous theme. Remind readers to share the pictures!

Questions for discussion:

■ *How many different colors can you find in "The Parade?" Is each animal a different color?*

■ *Look back through the stories from the theme and see whether you can find pictures that begin with /m/, /r/, or /s/.*

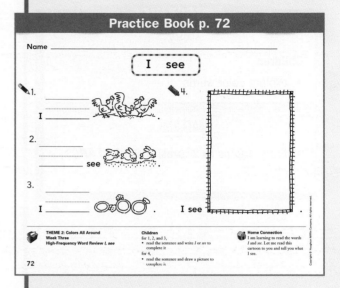

Practice Book p. 72

Portfolio Opportunity

Children may wish to add the Practice Book page to their portfolios as a sample of what they have learned.

Diagnostic Check

If...	You can...
children need help remembering the sound for consonant *r*,	have them listen to Reggie Rooster's song and listen for *r* words.

Word Work

Day 5

OBJECTIVES

Children

• explore color words

MATERIALS

• *From Apples to Zebras: A Book of ABC's,* page 29

Exploring Words

▶ Color Words

Remind children that they have been reading about and exploring colors.

■ Display *From Apples to Zebras: A Book of ABC's,* page 29. Call on volunteers to "read" the color words on the page.

■ After children have identified the colors, invite them to play a game of "I Spy" with you.

■ Page through the book, choosing a photograph, then display the pages. Describe the item you chose, using one or more color words but without naming the item, for example *I spy something red and white.* When most hands are up, have children identify the item.

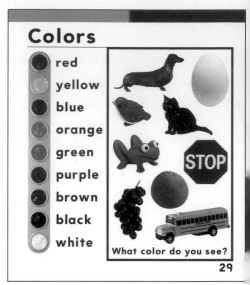

From Apples to Zebras: A Book of ABC's, **page 29**

■ As children feel comfortable, have them select a picture in the book and supply the clues to you or to a partner.

Independent Writing

▶ Journals

Review this week's shared and interactive writing posted in the classroom. Point out the naming word chart and the color charts. Invite children to discuss some of the things they learned during the theme. Tell them that today they will write about their favorite color activity.

- Pass out the journals.

- *This week we learned that some naming words name one person, place, or thing and others name more than one. What new words could you put in your journal?*

- *We also worked together to write chart the colors of the things we have read about. We even wrote a class summary. What were some of the colors of the things we read about?*

- Have children draw and write about their favorite color activity. Remind them that they can refer to classroom charts, the Word Wall, and the theme books as they write.

- If time permits, allow children to share what they've written with the class.

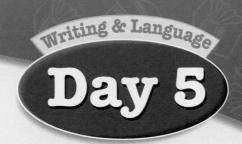
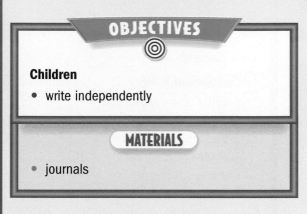

OBJECTIVES ◎

Children
- write independently

MATERIALS
- journals

Portfolio Opportunity

Mark journal entries you would like to share with parents. Allow children to choose their best efforts or favorite works for sharing as well.

DAY 5

Theme Assessment Wrap-Up

▶ **Monitoring Literacy Development**

If you have administered the **Emerging Literacy Survey** as a baseline assessment of the skills children brought with them to Kindergarten, this might be a good time to re-administer all or part of it, to chart progress, to identify areas of strength and need, and to test the need for early intervention.

Use the **Observation Checklist** throughout the theme to write notes indicating whether each child has a beginning, developing, or proficient understanding of reading, writing, and language concepts. (See facing page.)

▶ **Assessing Student Progress**

Formal Assessment The **Theme Skills Test** is a formal assessment used to evaluate children's performance on theme objectives.

- The **Theme Skills Test** assesses children's mastery of specific reading and language arts skills taught in the theme.

Emerging Literacy Survey

Areas Assessed:

1. **Concepts of Print**
   - Letter name knowledge
   - Sound-letter association
2. **Phonemic Awareness**
   - Rhyme
   - Beginning sounds
   - Blending onsets and rimes
   - Segmenting onsets and rimes
   - Blending phonemes
   - Segmenting phonemes
3. **Beginning Reading and Writing**
   - Word recognition
   - Word writing
   - Sentence dictation
   - Oral reading

Observation Checklist

Name _____   Date _____

	Beginning	Developing	Proficient
Listening Comprehension • Participates in shared and choral reading			
• Listens to story attentively			
Phonemic Awareness • Can identify beginning sounds			
• Can identify syllables in spoken words			
Phonics • Can recognize initial sounds *s, m, r*			
Concepts of Print • Recognizes use of capital at the beginning of a sentence			
• Can identify end punctuation			
Reading • Can read wordless stories			
• Can read the high-frequency words *I, see*			
Comprehension • Recognizes sequence of events			
• Can make inferences/ predictions			
Writing and Language • Can write simple words			
• Can participate in shared and interactive writing			

For each child, write notes or checkmarks in the appropriate columns.

Theme Resources
Resources for *Colors All Around*

Contents

Songs

Yankee Doodle

With spirit

Use this music for Sammy Seal's song.

This Old Man

Brightly, with spirit

Use this music for Mimi Mouse's song.

Hush! Little Baby

Use this music for Reggie Rooster's song.

Mary Wore Her Red Dress

Texas

Moderately Fast

Word List

In Themes 1 through 3, the Phonics Library stories are wordless.

Theme 1

▶ **Phonics Skills:** none taught in this theme
▶ **High-Frequency Words:** none taught in this theme

Phonics Library, Week 1:
We Go to School
wordless story

Phonics Library, Week 2:
See What We Can Do
wordless story

Phonics Library, Week 3:
We Can Make It
wordless story

Theme 2

▶ **Phonics Skills:** Initial consonants s, m, r
▶ **High-Frequency Words:** I, see

Phonics Library, Week 1:
My Red Boat
wordless story

Phonics Library, Week 2:
Look at Me
wordless story

Phonics Library, Week 3:
The Parade
wordless story

Theme 3

▶ **Phonics Skills:** Initial consonants t, b, n
▶ **High-Frequency Words:** my, like

Phonics Library, Week 1:
The Birthday Party
wordless story

Phonics Library, Week 2:
Baby Bear's Family
wordless story

Phonics Library, Week 3:
Cat's Surprise
wordless story

Theme 4

▶ **Phonics Skills:** Initial consonants h, v, c; words with -at
▶ **High-Frequency Words:** a, to

Phonics Library, Week 1:
Nat at Bat
   Words with *-at: at, bat, hat, Nat, sat*
   High-Frequency Words: *my, see*

Phonics Library, Week 2:
A Vat
   Words with *-at: hat, mat, rat, vat*
   High-Frequency Word: *a*

Phonics Library, Week 3:
Cat Sat
   Words with *-at: bat, cat, hat, mat, sat*
   High-Frequency Words: *my, see*

Theme 5

▶ **Phonics Skills:** Initial consonants p, g, f; words with -an
▶ **High-Frequency Words:** and, go

Phonics Library, Week 1:
Nat, Pat, and Nan
   Words with -an: *Nan, ran*
   Words with -at: *Nat, Pat, sat*
   High-Frequency Words: *and, see*

Phonics Library, Week 2:
Go, Cat!
   Words with *-an: Nan, ran, Van*
   Words with *-at: Cat, Pat, sat*
   High-Frequency Word: *go*

Phonics Library, Week 3:
Pat and Nan
   Words with *-an: fan, Nan, ran*
   Words with *-at: Pat, sat*
   High-Frequency Words: *a, and, go*

Theme 6

▶ **Phonics Skills:** Initial consonants l, k, qu; words with -it
▶ **High-Frequency Words:** is, here

Phonics Library, Week 1:
Can It Fit?
   Words with *-it: fit, it, sit*
   Words with *-an: can, man, van*
   High-Frequency Words: *a, go, I, is, my*

Phonics Library, Week 2:
Kit
   Words with *-it: bit, fit, it, Kit, lit, sit*
   Words with *-an: can, pan*
   Words with *-at: hat*
   High-Frequency Words: *a, here, I*

Phonics Library, Week 3:
Fan
   Words with *-it: bit, quit*
   Words with *-an: an, Fan*
   Words with *-at: sat*
   High-Frequency Words: *a, here, is*

Theme 7

▶ **Phonics Skills:** Initial consonants d, z; words with -ig
▶ **High-Frequency Words:** for, have

Phonics Library, Week 1:
Big Rig
   Words with *-ig: Big, dig, Rig*
   Words with *-it: pit*
   Words with *-an: can, Dan*
   High-Frequency Words: *a, for*

Phonics Library, Week 2:
Tan Van
   Words with *-ig: Pig, Zig*
   Words with *-it: it*
   Words with *-an: can, Dan, ran, tan, van*
   Words with *-at: Cat, sat*
   High-Frequency Words: *a, have, I, is*

Phonics Library, Week 3:
Zig Pig and Dan Cat
   Words with *-ig: dig, Pig, Zig*
   Words with *-it: it*
   Words with *-an: can, Dan*
   Words with *-at: Cat, sat*
   High-Frequency Words: *and, for, have, here, I, is*

Theme 8

▶ **Phonics Skills:** Consonant x; words with -ot, -ox

▶ **High-Frequency Words:** said, the

Phonics Library, Week 1:
Dot Got a Big Pot
Words with -ot: Dot, got, hot, lot, pot
Words with -ig: big
Words with -it: it
Words with -an: Nan
Words with -at: Nat, sat
High-Frequency Words: a, and, I, is, like, said

Phonics Library, Week 2:
The Big, Big Box
Words with -ox: box, Fox
Words with -ot: not
Words with -ig: big
Words with -it: bit, fit, hit, it
Words with -an: can, Dan, Fan
Words with -at: Cat, hat, mat, sat
High-Frequency Words: a, is, my, said, the

Phonics Library, Week 3:
A Pot for Dan Cat
Words with -ot: pot
Words with -ox: Fox
Words with -ig: big
Words with -it: fit
Words with -an: can, Dan, Fan, ran
Words with -at: Cat, sat
High-Frequency Words: a, and, see, said

Theme 9

▶ **Phonics Skills:** Initial consonants w, y; words with -et, -en

▶ **High-Frequency Words:** play, she

Phonics Library, Week 1:
Get Set! Play!
Words with -et: get, set, wet, yet
Words with -ot: got, not
Words with -ox: Fox
Words with -ig: Pig
Words with -an: can
High-Frequency Words: a, play, said

Phonics Library, Week 2:
Ben
Words with -en: Ben, Hen, men, ten
Words with -et: get, net, pet, vet, yet
Words with -ot: got, not
Words with -ox: box, Fox
Words with -it: it
Words with -an: can
High-Frequency Words: a, I, my, play, said, she, the

Phonics Library, Week 3:
Pig Can Get Wet
Words with -et: get, wet
Words with -ot: got, not
Words with -ig: big, Pig, wig
Words with -it: sit
Words with -an: can
Words with -at: Cat, sat
High-Frequency Words: a, my, play, said, she

Theme 10

▶ **Phonics Skills:** Initial consonant j; words with -ug, -ut

▶ **High-Frequency Words:** are, he

Phonics Library, Week 1:
Ken and Jen
Words with -ug: dug
Words with -en: Ken, Jen
Words with -et: wet
Words with -ot: hot
Words with -ig: big, dig
Words with -it: it, pit
High-Frequency Words: a, and, are, is

Phonics Library, Week 2:
It Can Fit
Words with -ut: but, nut
Words with -ug: jug, lug, rug
Words with -ox: box
Words with -ot: not
Words with -ig: big
Words with -it: fit, it
Words with -an: can, tan, van
Words with -at: fat, hat
High-Frequency Words: a, he, see, she

Phonics Library, Week 3:
The Bug Hut
Words with -ut: but
Words with -ug: Bug, hug, lug
Words with -ox: box
Words with -ot: Dot, got, not
Words with -ig: Big, jig
Words with -an: can, Jan
Words with -at: fat, hat
High-Frequency Words: a, here, is, she, the

Cumulative Word List

By the end of Theme 10, children will have been taught the skills necessary to read the following words.

Words with -at
at, bat, cat, fat, hat, mat, Nat, Pat, rat, sat, vat

Words with -an
an, ban, can, Dan, fan, Jan, man, Nan, pan, ran, tan, van

Words with -it
bit, fit, hit, it, kit, lit, pit, quit, sit, wit

Words with -ig
big, dig, fig, jig, pig, rig, wig, zig

Words with -ot
cot, dot, got, hot, jot, lot, not, pot, rot, tot

Words with -ox
box, fox, ox

Words with -et
bet, get, jet, let, met, net, pet, set, vet, wet, yet

Words with -en
Ben, den, hen, Jen, Ken, men, pen, ten

Words with -ug
bug, dug, hug, jug, lug, mug, rug, tug

Words with -ut
but, cut, hut, jut, nut, rut

High-Frequency Words
a, and, are, for, go, have, he, here, I, is, like, my, play, said, see, she, the, to

Technology Resources

American Melody
P. O. Box 270
Guilford, CT 06473
800-220-5557

Audio Bookshelf
174 Prescott Hill Road
Northport, ME 04849
800-234-1713

Baker & Taylor
100 Business Court Drive
Pittsburgh, PA 15205
800-775-2600

BDD Audio
1540 Broadway
New York, NY 10036
800-223-6834

Big Kids Productions
1606 Dywer Avenue
Austin, TX 78704
800-477-7811
www.bigkidsvideo.com

Blackboard Entertainment
2647 International
Boulevard
Suite 853
Oakland, CA 94601
800-968-2261
www.blackboardkids.com

Books on Tape
P. O. Box 7900
Newport Beach, CA 92658
800-626-3333

Filmic Archives
The Cinema Center
Botsford, CT 06404
800-366-1920
www.filmicarchives.com

Great White Dog Picture Company
10 Toon Lane
Lee, NH 03824
800-397-7641
www.greatwhitedog.com

HarperAudio
10 E. 53rd Street
New York, NY 10022
800-242-7737

Houghton Mifflin Company
222 Berkeley Street
Boston, MA 02116
800-225-3362

Informed Democracy
P. O. Box 67
Santa Cruz, CA 95063
831-426-3921

JEF Films
143 Hickory Hill Circle
Osterville, MA 02655
508-428-7198

Kimbo Educational
P. O. Box 477
Long Branch, NJ 07740
900-631-2187

**The Learning Company
(dist. for Broderbund)**
1 Athenaeum Street
Cambridge, MA 02142
800-716-8506
www.learningco.com

Library Video Co.
P. O. Box 580
Wynnewood, PA 19096
800-843-3620

Listening Library
One Park Avenue
Old Greenwich, CT 06870
800-243-45047

Live Oak Media
P. O. Box 652
Pine Plains, NY 12567
800-788-1121
liveoak@taconic.net

Media Basics
Lighthouse Square
P. O. Box 449
Guilford, CT 06437
800-542-2505
www.mediabasicsvideo.com

Microsoft Corp.
One Microsoft Way
Redmond, WA 98052
800-426-9400
www.microsoft.com

National Geographic Society
1145 17th Street N. W.
Washington, D. C. 20036
800-368-2728
www.nationalgeographic.com

New Kid Home Video
1364 Palisades Beach Road
Santa Monica, CA 90401
310-451-5164

Puffin Books
345 Hudson Street
New York, NY 10014
212-366-2000

Rainbow Educational Media
4540 Preslyn Drive
Raleigh, NC 27616
800-331-4047

Random House Home Video
201 E. 50th Street
New York, NY 10022
212-940-7620

Recorded Books
270 Skipjack Road
Prince Frederick, MD 20678
800-638-1304
www.recordedbooks.com

Sony Wonder
Dist. by Professional
Media Service
19122 S. Vermont Avenue
Gardena, CA 90248
800-223-7672

Spoken Arts
8 Lawn Avenue
P. O. Box 100
New Rochelle, NY 10802
800-326-4090

SRA Media
220 E. Danieldale Road
DeSoto, TX 75115
800-843-8855

Sunburst Communications
101 Castleton Street
P. O. Box 100
Pleasantville, NY 10570
800-321-7511
www.sunburst.com

SVE & Churchill Media
6677 North Northwest
Highway
Chicago, IL 60631
800-829-1900

Tom Snyder Productions
80 Coolidge Hill Road
Watertown, MA 02472
800-342-0236
www.tomsnyder.com

Troll Communications
100 Corporate Drive
Mahwah, NJ 07430
800-526-5289

Weston Woods
12 Oakwood Avenue
Norwalk, CT 06850-1318
800-243-5020
www.scholastic.com

Index

Boldface page references indicate formal strategy and skill instruction.

N

Newsletters. *See* Home connection.

Nouns. *See* Speech, parts of.

O

On My Way Practice Readers
    Beautiful Butterflies by Demaris Tyler,
      T108, T153

Onset and rime. *See* Phonemic
awareness.

Oral composition. *See* Speaking activities.

Oral language development, *T10–T11,
T15, T18–T19, T62–T63, T69, T94,
T116–T117, T123, T126–T127,
T136–T137*

Oral Reading Fluency. *See* Fluency,
reading.

Oral summary. *See* Summarizing.

P

Parent involvement. *See* Home
connection.

Personal response. *See* Responding to
literature.

Phonemic awareness
    beginning sounds, **T9, T12–T13, T17,
      T20, T27, T34, T39, T42, T47, T61,
      T66, T71, T74, T81, T88, T93, T96,
      T101, T115, T120, T125, T128,
      T135, T138, T146, T151**
    blending onset and rime, **T143**
    syllables in spoken words, counting,
      **T9, T17, T27, T39, T47, T61, T71,
      T81, T93, T96, T101, T115, T125,
      T135, T151**
    words in oral sentences, **T143**

**Phonics, *T6, T13, T21, T43, T58, T67, T75,
T97, T112, T121, T129, T147***

consonants, initial
    b, **T61**

m, **T66, T67, T71, T74, T75, T88,
    T89, T92, T96, T97, T99, T101,
    T104, T121, T128, T147, T154**
r, **T115, T120, T121, T125, T128,
    T129, T138, T146–T147, T151,
    T154, T155**
s, **T20–T21, T27, T34, T35, T42–T43,
    T47, T50, T74, T97, T99, T104,
    T121, T128, T147, T154**

Phonics Library titles
    Look at Me, *T89, T103*
    My Red Boat, *T3, T35, T43, T48, T49*
    The Parade, *T109, T139, T147,
      T152, T155*

Phonological awareness. *See* Phonemic
awareness.

Predicting. *See* Comprehension skills.

Predictions, making and checking
    from previewing, *T10, T18, T29,
      T126, T145*
    while reading, *T28, T62, T94*

Print awareness. *See* Concepts of print.

Punctuation. *See* Concepts of print.

R

Read Aloud selections
    Caps of Many Colors, *T54, T62–T65,
      T102*
    *How the Birds Got Their Colors,
      T108, T116–T119, T152*
    I Need a Lunch Box by Jeannette
      Caines, ill. by Pat Cummings, *T2,
      T10, T11, T48*

Reading fluency. *See* Fluency.

Reading log. *See* Journal.

Reading modes
    guided reading, *T153*
    oral reading, *T49, T76, T103*
    teacher read aloud, *T2, T10, T11,
      T19, T54, T62–T65, T108,
      T116–T119*
    See also Rereading.

Reading strategies. *See* Strategies,
reading.

Reference and study skills
    graphic sources. *See* Graphic informa-
      tion, interpreting.

Rereading
    for comprehension, *T28, T82, T126,
      T137*
    orally, *T49, T103, T126*

Responding to literature, options for
    discussion, *T19, T33, T48, T86,
      T102, T145, T152*
    personal response, *T19, T73, T144*

Retelling
    story, *T33, T86*

Routines
    daily, *T4–T5, T56–T57, T110–T111*
    instructional, *xiv*
    management, *xv*
    opening, *T8–T9, T16–T17, T26–T27,
      T46–T47, T70–T71, T80–T81,
      T92–T93, T100–T101,
      T114–T115, T124–T125,
      T134–T135, T142–T143,
      T150–T151*

S

Science activities. *See* Cross-curricular
links.

Sentence building, *T68, T76, T78,
T105, T122, T124, T132, T155*

Sequence of events, noting. *See*
Comprehension skills.

**Shared writing, *T36, T45, T91, T141,
T149***

Sight words. *See* High-frequency words.

Skills links
    science, *iv, T3, T40–T41, T55, T94,
      T144–T145*

Speaking activities
    describe people, places, things,
      number words, *T91*